CLASSIC TEXTS IN
MUSIC EDUCATION 25

ELEMENTS OF MUSICAL COMPOSITION

CLASSIC TEXTS IN MUSIC EDUCATION

Continued at the back of the book

Wm Crotch

ELEMENTS OF MUSICAL COMPOSITION
Second edition
(1830)

Introduced by
Bernarr Rainbow

Reproduced under the direction
of Leslie Hewitt for
BOETHIUS PRESS
Aberystwyth, Wales

British Library Cataloguing in Publication Data

Crotch, William *1775-1847*
Elements of musical composition.—
(Classic texts in music education, v. 25).
1. Music. Composition
I. Title II. Rainbow, Bernarr III. Series
781.3
ISBN 0-86314-122-6

The publishers thank Dr Bernarr Rainbow
for lending his copy for reprinting

Photographed and printed
BOETHIUS PRESS
3 The Science Park
Aberystwyth, Wales

INTRODUCTION

For the eighteenth-century English musician—and William Crotch was essentially that—a successful career embraced performing, teaching, and composing. But during the second half of the century as general educational and cultural standards among native musicians improved, a few leading figures began tentatively to explore the additional field of musical scholarship; publications relating to aesthetic, historical and scientific aspects of music started to appear. And as this new generation of articulate musicians— Avison, Burney, Arnold, Busby and Callcott among them—began in their several ways to rediscover the fascination of publicly discussing as well as making music, the vanished distinction between practical musician and theorist, formerly so evident as to call for the definition 'practicall and speculative' on the title pages of Elizabethan treatises, regained currency in England once more. Moreover, the writings of these men not infrequently outweighed their musical compositions in value; and as in other fields the specialist was soon seen to outshine, then eclipse, the general practitioner.

As a latecomer to this scene William Crotch (1775-1847) seems in some ways to contradict the trend. For though he lived on well into Victoria's reign he retained all the universality of the eighteenth-century musician as performer, teacher and composer; managing though to supplement without reducing those characteristics by being the first professor of music in England in modern times to deliver expository lectures within his university and to publish a comprehensive treatise elucidating written musical skills for the guidance of students generally.

Examination of Crotch's principal writings perhaps resolves the paradox—for whether he is discussing the history of music, as in *The Substance of Several Courses of Lectures* (1831), the realisation of figured basses, in *Practical Thorough Bass* (1825), or advanced written skills, in *Elements of Musical Composition* (1812), the result can clearly be seen as an unaffected extension of his activity as a teacher rather than a pursuit of scholarship for its own sake. The same attitude is demonstrated yet more evidently in some of his minor publications. *Questions in Harmony, with their Answers, for the Examination of Young Pupils*, for instance, leaves no doubt as to its essentially practical purpose; and even in the field of composition such a title as *Thirty Rounds for the Piano-forte for learning to play from Score*, makes plain the humble pedagogical object for which these 'learned' pieces were written.

As a result, Crotch's essential geniality often shines out irrepressibly from his pages. Even in so cheerless a context as the rules governing part-writing he manages to interpolate a few warming footnotes:

> Several composers (generally however from oversight) have left violations of these rules in their works. Domenico Scarlatti was perhaps the only one who professedly disregarded them for the sake of producing good effects. But whatever may have been the success of this great master, the passages in which he has transgressed the rules do not appear to have become the object of imitation in other composers. (*infra*, p.23)

And having emphasised the ban on consecutive fifths as 'the most strict rule of any in music' he adds a relenting sequel:

> The author has not directed his pupils to avoid what are called hidden 5ths and 8ves, as he finds no composers observe these rules since the period of writing plain counterpoint in only two parts. (*infra*, p.25)

Unprecedented leniency of this order is justified by investigation of authentic practice in former times—the 'scholarly' nature of which he avoids stressing.

Crotch's *Elements of Musical Composition* (1812), reproduced here from the second edition of 1833, is an essentially practical work whose first aim is to equip pianist and organist to fulfil their accompanimental roles. As such, after summarising musical rudiments many of its pages are devoted to detailed guidance on the realisation of figured basses. Tightly compressed and overtly transmitting 'the accumulated experience of many treatises' the text of this section of the book consists largely of 'rules'. But many illustrative examples are given, selected from the works of Handel, J. C. Bach, Purcell, Corelli, Wagenseil, Pergolesi, Hasse and Haydn; equally, exceptions to the stated rules found in the compositions of Haydn, Mozart and Rossini are acknowledged, and the reader is urged to consult the works of 'good composers' for himself, adopting whatever he admires in their procedures.

The importance of 'a very good ear and taste' is stressed. And an unusual device which Crotch introduces to assist the beginner to 'hear' the notes of individual chords as they are described on the page deserves special mention. From the outset, Crotch uses sol-fa to designate both intervals and chord structures, employing the Italian spelling and a movable *do*. He thus states the procedure for resolving the chord of the dominant seventh in these terms: the discordant note must fall—Fa to Mi; the leading note must rise—Si to Do; Re may go to Do; and Sol, if in the bass, should either fall to Do, or stand still. All that separates his use of sol-fa from later orthodoxy is his preference for retaining Do as the tonic in minor keys.

Turning to the treatment of counterpoint—a topic first introduced in the chapter on 'Melody'—Crotch promptly dismisses antique procedures:

> The rules of counterpoint are not given in this work, as they seem to have become obsolete. (*infra*, p.30)

Cherubini's systematic *Cours de contrepoint et de fugue* (1835), drawn up for the Paris Conservatoire and based on the work of earlier theorists still lay in the future when Crotch's treatise appeared. And his own interpretation of the term seems limited to the harmonic counterpoint of the baroque era. The student is introduced to the subject by writing canons of all kinds, including the more abstruse varieties which clearly fascinated Crotch and occupied much of his leisure in later life. A surprisingly short account of fugal structure follows, but it is copiously illustrated by varied musical examples. Once again, sol-fa is employed to help clarify the relationships existing between Subject and Answer:

> In the commencement of a strict fugue, the extreme notes Do and Sol of the authentic mode are to be respectively answered by the extreme notes Sol and Do of the plagal, the intermediate notes not being liable to any rule.

> Thus Do is answered by Sol
> Re ” ” ” La
> Mi ” ” ” Si (*infra*, p.77)

For his first attempts at original composition, as opposed to the working of exercises, the student is required to write plain series of chords such as might be elaborated into quasi-improvised preludes. Detailed guidance is left to personal discussions between master and pupil. But what now seems very elementary advice follows on the use of voices and instruments—incidentally casting revealing light upon the extreme youth and naiveté of Crotch's pupils, especially in his days as a teacher at the newly-founded Royal Academy of Music:

> In composing for key-board instruments, the number of notes which the hand can grasp should be considered...In composing for stringed instruments, such chords, or double stops, must not be used as cannot be executed. (*infra*, pp. 82-83)

In such problematical areas the young composer is advised to acquire more detailed knowledge either by consulting a performer or by avoiding what cannot be found in 'the works of the great composers'.

With this basic equipment the novice is recommended to proceed to writing madrigals and quartets. The former exercise will entail providing real parts for voices in the ancient style; the latter, for instruments and in the modern style. Added to this he should write variations 'in the manner of different masters' both upon well-known airs and ground basses. After that, all that remains is for him to 'form his taste by the study of various styles of music'— a discipline beyond the scope of the present volume whose aim has been limited to equipping the student to write 'with grammatical correctness'.

As its reappearance in a new edition in 1833 suggests, Crotch's *Elements* enjoyed long popularity and influence among students. Only when an English version of Cherubini's *Cours de contrepoint et fugue* appeared in 1841 was Crotch's book replaced by it at the Royal Academy of Music in London. But by that time other changes had taken place in what had too largely been an ultra-conservative institution; and the teaching of composition was revolutionised there by Crotch's successor, Cipriani Potter—an underestimated figure today—whose understanding of symphonic structure, orchestration and the true role of the piano as a solo instrument made him the most influential teacher of his day and the founder of a new school of English composers.

It was in preparing and breaking the soil for that new phase in English music that the importance of William Crotch's contribution as teacher and writer may be said to rest.

NOTE: In the original, the page numbering of text and musical illustrations duplicated the same series. To avoid confusion, new page numbers running throughout have been added in square brackets.

ELEMENTS OF MUSICAL COMPOSITION

Plate II.

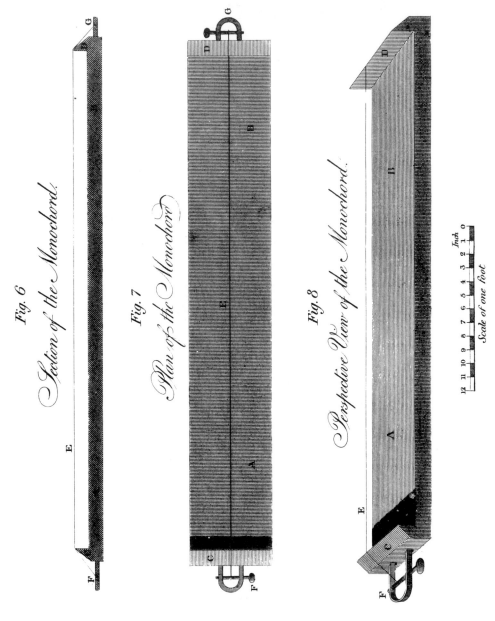

Fig. 6

Section of the Monochord.

Fig. 7

Plan of the Monochord.

Fig. 8

Perspective View of the Monochord.

Scale of one foot

[2]

ELEMENTS

OF

MUSICAL COMPOSITION;

COMPREHENDING THE

RULES OF THOROUGH BASS

AND THE

Theory of Tuning.

BY WILLIAM CROTCH, Mus. Doc.,

PROFESSOR OF MUSIC IN THE UNIVERSITY OF OXFORD.

SECOND EDITION.

LONDON:

LONGMAN, REES, ORME, BROWN, GREEN, AND LONGMAN,

PATERNOSTER-ROW.

MDCCCXXXIII.

LONDON:
Printed by WILLIAM CLOWES,
Duke-street, Lambeth.

PREFACE TO THE FIRST EDITION.

A KNOWLEDGE of the Elements of Musical Composition and of Thorough Bass is happily become almost indispensable to a Musical Education.

The present work was at first intended for the author's pupils, but is now published with the hope that it may become more generally useful.

Originality seldom forms the leading feature of a work of this nature, the excellence of which should consist chiefly in the accumulated experience of many treatises. Those already published have been consulted, but their language has not, intentionally at least, been adopted. They have contributed materially to such parts of this work as may be found to possess any merit; and for the rest the author wishes he could offer a better recommendation than novelty.

No. 2, Duchess Street, Jan. 6, 1812.

PREFACE TO THE SECOND EDITION.

THE demand for a second Edition of this work is gratefully acknowledged by the author, and has induced him to make many additions and alterations, and to correct the errors and imperfections of the former edition, as far as he has been able to detect them.

No. 10, Holland Street, Kensington, October, 1833.

CONTENTS.

CHAPTER I.

CHAPTER II.

CHAPTER III.

CHAPTER IV.

CHAPTER V.

CHAPTER VI.

[9]

CHAPTER VII.

CHAPTER VIII.

CHAPTER IX.

Plate I.

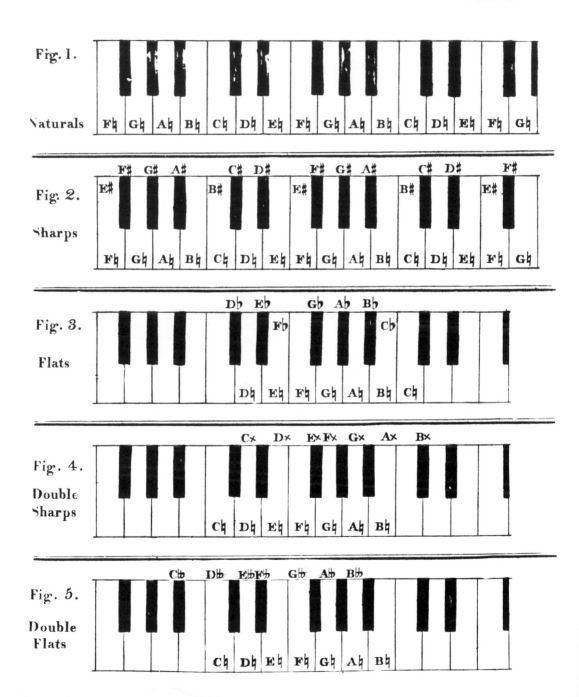

ELEMENTS

OF

MUSICAL COMPOSITION.

CHAPTER I.

OF NOTES, INTERVALS, SCALES, AND KEYS.

A NOTE or single sound, whether produced by one or more strings, pipes, voices, or instruments, is called a unison. Twelve different notes are produced by the seven white and five black keys of a keyed instrument*, not including the repetitions of notes of the same name, higher or lower, called their octaves. The difference of pitch between any two notes is called an interval. The smallest interval, as from any note to the next above or below it, is called a semitone. A tone is the distance from any note to the next but one, above or below it, and is equal to two semitones. Notes are either naturals, sharps, flats, double sharps, or double flats.

The seven white keys are generally naturals, and are then called, A♮ B♮ C♮ D♮ E♮ F♮ G♮. See fig. 1, plate I.

---

* The organ and piano-forte are the only instruments now in general use, to which the term *keyed instrument* is meant to be applied in this work.

B

[13]

A sharp is one semitone higher than the natural of the same name. Thus A♯ is one semitone higher than A♮, and is a black key lying between A♮ and B♮. See fig. 2: and thus B♯ is a white key otherwise called C♮.

A flat is one semitone lower than a natural. Thus A♭ is the black note lying between A♮ and G♮. See fig. 3: C♭ is a white key, otherwise called B♮.

A double sharp is a whole tone above a natural. Thus A𝄪 is the white key, otherwise called B♮.

B𝄪 is the black key, otherwise called C♯ or D♭. See fig. 4.

A double flat is a whole tone below a natural. Thus A♭♭ is the white key otherwise called G♮: and F♭♭ is the black key otherwise called E♭ or D♯. See fig. 5.

Thorough bass is the expressing of notes by figures reckoning upwards from the bass. The figures used are 2, 3, 4, 5, 6, 7, 8, and 9*.

A second signifies the next note above or below, according to alphabetical order. Thus the second to† A is B, whether natural, flat, or sharp; and that, either the next in position, or in any other octave above it. Thus any B♮ B♭ or B♯ above a given A is called second to it, excepting when written as a ninth. And thus any G♮ G♭ or G♯ below A is called the second below A♮.

---

* 1 is not used, being a unison. 10, 11, 12, &c., are not used, because they are double figures. **3** stands for **3** or **10**; **4**, for **4** or **11**, &c.—See the Author's *Practical Thorough Bass*, and his *Questions and Answers for Young Students*.

† The second *to* any note signifies the second *above* it, all intervals being reckoned upwards, from the bass, or lowest note, unless when specified to the contrary. In thorough bass the figures are always reckoned upwards. Seconds, thirds, &c., are improperly called intervals; they are notes. Their distance from any other note is the interval.

A, in this work, stands for A ♮, B for B ♮, &c.

A third is the third note inclusive, or next note but one, above or below. Thus the 3rd to A is C, and the 3rd below A is F.

	4th	..	D,	..	4th	..	E.
..	5th	..	E,	..	5th	..	D.
..	6th	..	F,	..	6th	..	C.
..	7th	..	G,	..	7th	..	B.
..	8th, or octave	A,	..	8th	..	A.
..	9th	..	B,	..	9th	..	G.

A Scale is a succession of notes repeated an octave higher or lower to an indefinite distance, only terminating with the compass of the instrument.

A Diatonic Scale consists of five tones and two semitones, the latter being separated by two tones and three tones alternately; and the notes being in alphabetical order. See Example 1.

The intervals contained between the notes of this scale are, in this work, called Diatonic Intervals; and are as follow:

Two kinds of 2nd—a minor 2nd equal to 1 semitone, as from E to F
a major 2nd .. 2 semitones, . F to G
Two kinds of 3rd—a minor 3rd* .. 3 . . A to C
a major 3rd † .. 4 . . . C to E
Two kinds of 4th—a perfect 4th .. 5 . . C to F
a superfluous 4th ‡ .. 6 . . F to B
Two kinds of 5th—an imperfect 5th § .. 6 . . . B to F
a perfect 5th .. 7 . . C to G

* Called also a flat third, or lesser third.

† Called also a sharp third, or greater third.

‡ Called also the extreme sharp 4th, and Tritonus, from the three successive tones FG, GA, and AB, of which it is composed. Sometimes also it is called imperfect.

§ Called also the extreme flat, or false 5th.

B 2

[15]

Two kinds of 6th—a minor 6th   ..   8 semitones, as from E to C

a major 6th   ..   9   .   .   C to A

Two kinds of 7th—a minor 7th*   ..   10   .   .   .   G to F

a major 7th†   ..   11   .   .   C to B

One kind of 8th, or octave,   ..   12   .   .   .   C to C

Two kinds of 9th—a minor 9th   ..   13   .   .   B to C

a major 9th   ..   14   .   .   .   C to D

See Example 2.

A Chromatic Scale signifies, in this work‡, one in which the semitones are placed in any way differently from those in the Diatonic Scale: as

$$A \quad B \quad C \quad D \quad E \quad F \quad G\sharp \quad A$$
$$T \quad\; S \quad\; T \quad\; T \quad\; S \quad T\&\tfrac{1}{2} \quad S$$

Or,
$$A \quad B \quad C \quad D \quad E \quad F\sharp \quad G\sharp \quad A$$
$$T \quad\; S \quad\; T \quad\; T \quad\; T \quad\; T \quad\; S$$

See example 3.

Chromatic Intervals signify, in this work, those peculiar to the Chromatic Scale; such are

An extreme sharp 2nd equal to 3 semitones, as from F to G$\sharp$

..   flat   3rd   ..   2   ....   B to D$\flat$

..   flat   4th   ..   4   ....   B to E$\flat$

..   sharp   5th   ..   8   ....   C to G$\sharp$

..   sharp   6th   ..   10   .,..   C to A$\sharp$

---

* Called also a flat 7th.   † Called also a sharp 7th.

‡ The Chromatic and Enharmonic Scales of the Grecians are to us unintelligible. But it is very remarkable that as the white keys of our instruments give the true Diatonic Scale of the Ancients, so the black keys, when used alone, give a species of Enharmonic Scale found in Chinese and Javanese music, and in some of the Irish and Scotch national airs.

An extreme flat   7th equal to 9* semitones, as from B to A♭

  ..   flat 8ve.   ..   11   ....   c to c♭

  ..   sharp 8ve.   ..   13   ....   c to c♯

  ..   sharp 9th   ..   15   ....   c to D♯

See Example 4.

An Enharmonic scale contains smaller intervals than semitones, as quarter tones, commas, &c. which cannot be distinguished on a keyed instrument. See Example 5.

Enharmonic intervals signify such as are peculiar to the Enharmonic Scale. See Example 6.

The Inversion of an interval is its complement, or what is remaining to complete the octave. It is found by changing the place of the two notes which form it, putting the lowest above the other, or the highest below.

Thus the inversion of $\frac{B}{A}$ is $\frac{A}{B}$. The inversion of $\frac{F}{C}$ is $\frac{C}{F}$ &c.

Thus a 2nd inverted is a   7th

          3rd 6th

          4th 5th

          5th 4th

          6th 3rd

And a 7th 2nd

Hence also it follows, that a 5th above is the same note as a 4th below; a 3rd above as a 6th below; and a 2nd above as a 7th below. Also that a 5th below is the same note as a 4th above; a 3rd below as a 6th above; and a 2nd below as a 7th above.

* Chromatic semitones, as distinct from diatonic semitones, are not noticed in this part of the work, because they are not distinguishable on keyed instruments; but they will be noticed in the articles Tuning, Temperament, &c.

[17]

A minor interval inverted .   .   becomes major

A major .   .   .   .   .   minor

A perfect   .   .   .   remains perfect

An imperfect   .   .   .   .   imperfect

An extreme sharp   .   becomes extreme flat

And an extreme flat   .   .   .   extreme sharp

Thus, a minor 2nd inverted   .   becomes a major 7th

a major 6th   .   .   .   .   a minor 3rd

a perfect 4th   .   .   .   .   a perfect 5th

an imperfect or superfluous 4th   .   an imperfect 5th

an extreme sharp 5th   .   .   an extreme flat 4th

and an extreme flat 4th   .   .   an extreme sharp 5th

See Example 7.

A key, or mode, consists of seven notes, arranged in alphabetical order, called

The key note	Tonic, or	.	.	.	Do *
2nd	Supertonic, or	.	.	.	Re
3rd	Mediant, or	.	.	.	Mi
4th	Subdominant, or	.	.	.	Fa †
5th	Dominant, or	.	.		Sol

* In this work, as in some others, Do is the key note, Re the 2d, &c. whatever the key may be, but in France, Re always signifies D; Mi, E, &c.

† The Subdominant is so called from its being the 5th below the key note, as the Dominant is the 5th above. The Dominant is so called from its predominance in Music, being common to the Triads of Do and Sol, and more frequently used than any other note. Do is likewise common to the Triads of Do and Fa, but the triad of Fa is not so often used as that of Sol. Fa is also often used with a $\frac{6}{3}$, Do being omitted.

The 6th note Submediant, or . . . La *

7th   Leading Note, Subtonic, or   Si †

Keys are either major or minor. They are so called according as the 3rd to the key note is major or minor.

In the major key, the intervals, if reckoned from the key note, are all either major or perfect.

Thus, from Do to Re is a major 2nd

....   Mi is a major 3rd

....   Fa is a perfect 4th

....   Sol is a perfect 5th

....   La is a major 6th

....   Si is a major 7th

....   Do is a perfect 8th

The major key is Diatonic.

From Do to Re is a . tone

.. Re to Mi   tone

.. Mi to Fa   semitone

.. Fa to Sol . tone

.. Sol to La . . tone

.. La to Si . tone

.. Si to Do   semitone

* The Submediant is the 3rd below the key note, as the Mediant is the 3rd above. The Mediant is the middle note between Do and Sol, as the Submediant is between Do and the Fa below it.

† It is called the leading note, (when placed at the distance of one semitone below the key note, as is usually the case,) because it generally leads to the key note, *viz.* is succeeded by it; and the French call it the *sensible* note, as that whereby the key is known. When placed a whole tone below the key note, Si should not be called the leading note, but the flat 7th of the key, or subtonic.

[19]

Viz. two tones and a semitone, and three tones and a semitone; see page 3 and example 8, as in the major key of C, which has no flats or sharps. Other major keys are formed on any key note by a similar arrangement of tones and semitones; and, if placed according to the numerical order of their flats and sharps, their key notes will be at the distance of a perfect 5th from each other. Thus G major, which has one sharp, is a 5th above C; D, which has two sharps, is a 5th above G; F with one flat is a 5th below C; B♭ with two flats is a 5th below F, &c. &c. as in the following table.

FLATS.											SHARPS.													
10	9	8*	7	6	5	4	3	2	1	0	1	2	3	4	5	6	7*	8	9	10	11	12	13	14
Ebb	Bbb	Fb	Cb	Gb	Db	Ab	Eb	Bb	F	C	G	D	A	E	B	F♯	C♯	G♯	D♯	A♯	E♯	B♯	F♯♯	C♯♯, &c.

See Example 9.

Keys which have more than seven sharps or flats are very seldom used†.

The ancient‡ diatonic minor key has a minor 3rd, minor 6th, and minor 7th. The other intervals being the same as in the major key.

Thus from *Do* to *Re* § is a major 2nd
. . . .   *Mi*   . .   minor 3rd
. . . .   *Fa*   . .   perfect 4th
. . . .   *Sol* . .   perfect 5th

* Keys which have more than seven sharps or flats, have double sharps or flats, which reckon for two.

† Major keys in modern music, as well as minor keys, have occasional accidental flats and sharps, which will hereafter be noticed.

‡ So called, in this work, from its being the scale of the ancient Greek Music, and found in the oldest national tunes, in psalms, and cathedral music; see Specimens of various kinds of Music, vol. i. No. 13, page 14, No. 24, page 19, and vol. ii. No. 6, page 2. It is also represented by the first seven letters of the alphabet, which seems to imply that those who gave these names to this mode considered it as the primary one.

§ The syllables *Do, Re,* &c. are put in italics in the minor key to distinguish them from those of the major key. They are also distinguished by a line drawn under them.

[20]

Thus from $\underline{Do}$ to $\underline{La}$ .. minor 6th

.... $\overline{Si}$ .. minor 7th

And thus from $\overline{Do}$ to $\overline{Re}$ is a tone

.... $\overline{Re}$ to $\overline{Mi}$ .. semitone

.... $\overline{Mi}$ to $\overline{Fa}$ .. tone

.... $\overline{Fa}$ to $\overline{Sol}$ .. tone

.... $\overline{Sol}$ to $\overline{La}$ .. semitone

.... $\overline{La}$ to $\overline{Si}$ .. tone

.... $\overline{Si}$ to $\overline{Do}$ .. tone

Viz. five tones and two semitones, the latter being separated by two tones and three tones alternately, which constitutes a Diatonic Scale, as in the minor key of A which has no flats or sharps. See Example 10.

Other minor keys are formed on any key note by a similar arrangement of tones and semitones; and if placed according to the numerical order of their flats and sharps, their key notes will be at the distance of a perfect 5th from each other. Thus E minor has one sharp; B, two sharps; D, one flat, &c. as in the following table. See Example 11.

FLATS. SHARPS.

13	12	11	10	9	8	7	6	5	4	3	2	1	0	1	2	3	4	5	6	7	8	9	10	11
E♭♭	B♭♭	F♭	C♭	G♭	D♭	A♭	E♭	B♭	F	C	G	D	A	E	B	F♯	C♯	G♯	D♯	A♯	E♯	B♯	F♯♯	C♯♯, &c.

The sixth note $\underline{La}$ and the seventh $\underline{Si}$ are occasionally[*] raised one semitone. If the sixth is raised, (and not the seventh,) an ancient diatonic minor key is produced, now become obsolete. See Example 12, and Specimens, vol. i. No. 66, page 40.

In modern music, the seventh note $\underline{Si}$ is often made one semitone higher,

[*] These alterations are only occasional, and the sharps or naturals requisite to produce them are accidental, and not marked at the beginning of the piece. The third note of the minor key is sometimes also altered. See note, page 14.

and then the scale of the minor key becomes chromatic.   See example 13, and Specimens, vol. i. No. 278 and 279, page 136.

The sixth and seventh notes are both occasionally altered at the same time, and then also the scale is chromatic.   See Example 14, and Specimens, vol. i. No. 161, page 84.

This is the usual method of ascending the minor key, but in descending, the ancient diatonic scale is commonly used.   See Example 15, and Specimens, vol. i. last two bars of No. 130, page 69*.

* The melody of the minor key depends, however, in a great measure, on the harmony.

CHAPTER II.

OF CONCORDS.

HARMONY is a succession of Chords*, either fully expressed, or partly understood.

A Chord is a coincidence of sounds, and is either a concord or a discord.

A Concord is a coincidence of two, or at most of three different notes, none of which are next to each other, as to their alphabetical order†, and none of which form an extreme flat or sharp interval.

Thus E   G A   F, &c. are concords.   D   F G B   D G, &c. are discords.

Thus
     G A
  E F, &c. are concords.
    C D

    F G B
  D D G, &c. are discords.
  B C F

A triad is any note accompanied with its third and fifth. Consonant triads are such as have no imperfect interval; or, in other words, such as are concords. In Dissonant triads the fifths are not perfect, and they are consequently discords‡. A major triad is so called from its third being major, and a minor triad from its third being minor.

---

* It has been objected to this definition, that a single concord produces harmony, but I have retained it, as no piece of music consists of only one chord.

† G A are included in this order, the musical alphabet ending with G, and, if produced, standing thus, A B C D E F G A B C &c.

‡ Dissonant triads, such as
    F   C♯
    D   A, &c. will be treated of hereafter.
    B   F

There are six consonant triads in a diatonic scale, and one dissonant.

Thus in the scale of naturals

	G	A	B	C	D	E	
	E	F	G	A	B	C	are consonant triads.
	C	D	E	F	G	A	

F
D is dissonant.   The triad is called by the name of its lowest note.   Thus
B

G   D
E is the triad of C, and the triad of G is B, &c.
C   G

Of the above six triads three are major and three minor.   The triads of C, F, and G, are major; those of D, E, and A, are minor.

Every diatonic scale, on a keyed instrument*, may be considered as comprehending two keys, the one major and the other minor, both having the same number of flats and sharps.   Thus the scale of naturals includes the keys of C major and A minor.   A scale with one sharp includes G major and E minor.   A scale with three flats includes E♭ major, and C minor, &c., and this minor key is called relative minor to the major key ; and the major key, relative major to the minor key.

The three major triads belong to the major key, and the three minor triads to the minor key, and are the triads of Do, Fa, and Sol in each.

Thus in the scale of naturals the triads of C, F, and G, belong to the major key of C, and are the triads of Do, Fa, and Sol ; and the triads of A, D, and E, belong to the minor key of A, and are the triads of *Do, Fa,* and *Sol.*   See Example 16.

---

* But this is only the case on keyed instruments, for nature requires smaller intervals than semitones for the union of a major and its relative minor key, which, therefore, constitutes a kind of enharmonic scale.

DIATONIC SCALES.

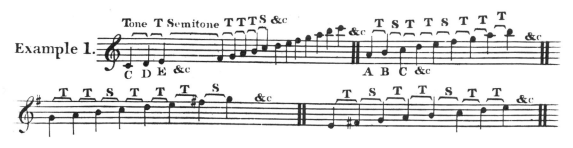

DIATONIC INTERVALS.

CHROMATIC SCALES.

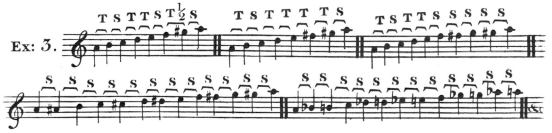

CHROMATIC INTERVALS.

ENHARMONIC SCALES.

Ex:5.

ENHARMONIC INTERVALS.

Ex:6.

INVERSION OF INTERVALS.

Ex:7.

A Major 2d. A Minor 7th. A Major 3d. A Minor 6th. A perfect 4th. A perfect 5th.

A Minor 3d. A Major 6th. An imperfect or extreme sharp 4th. An imperfect or extreme flat 5th.

The Major Key of C.

Ex:8.

Do the key note or Tonic. Re the 2d. or Supertonic. Mi the 3d. or Mediant.

Fa the 4th. or Subdominant. Sol the 5th. or Dominant. La the 6th. or Submediant. Si the 7th. Leading note or Subtonic.

Tonic Mediant Dominant Submediant Subdominant Supertonic Subtonic

4

The Minor Key of A.

Ex:10.

A Major 2d | A Minor 3d | A perfect 4th | A perfect 5th | A Minor 6th | A Min. 7th

E Minor. Ex:11.

Do Re Mi Fa Sol La Si Do

B Minor.   F# Minor.

Do Re Mi Fa Sol La Si Do

C# Minor.   D Minor.

Do Re Mi Fa Sol La Si Do &c

G Minor.   C Minor.

Do Re Mi Fa Sol La Si Do

F Minor.

Do Re Mi Fa Sol La Si Do

AN OBSOLETE DIATONIC MINOR SCALE

Ex: 12.

Do Re Mi Fa Sol La Si Do

A CHROMATIC MINOR SCALE

Ex: 13.

Do Re Mi Fa Sol La Si Do

ANOTHER CHROMATIC MINOR SCALE

Ex: 14.

Do Re Mi Fa Sol La Si Do

THE USUAL MANNER OF ASCENDING & DESCENDING THE MINOR KEY

Ex: 15.

Do Re Mi Fa Sol La Si Do Si La Sol Fa Mi Re Do

6

⊕ In thorough bass a 3ᵈ. is always understood & to be performed when a 4ᵗʰ. or a 2ⁿᵈ. is not expressed ___ thus 6 stands for $\frac{6}{3}$ ___ $\frac{6}{5}$ when followed by $\frac{6}{4}$ however, must not have a 3.
✳ Tasto Solo in thoro' bass signifies that no chords are to be played.

* The syllables **Do Fa or Solare** (in this work) written under inverfions as well as direct **harmony** &
are intended to shew, not the name of the bass note but of the fundamental note or root of the chord.

✳ $\frac{6}{3}$ is usually written 6. a 3 being understood where neither 4 nor 2 is put. See
note ⊕ on Page 7.

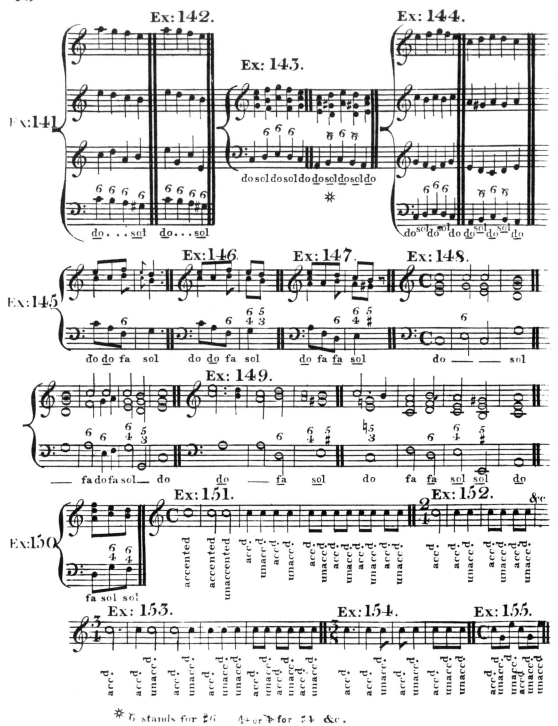

As thus in C major

C	G	D
A	E	B
F	C	G
Fa	Do	Sol

And thus in A minor

A	E	B
F	C	G
D	A	E
Fa	*Do*	*Sol*

They are placed in this order because *Fa* the subdominant is the 5th below *Do*, as *Sol* the dominant is the 5th above.

Hence it appears that a key consists of a key note with its third and fifth, together with the key notes next to it (*viz.*, the dominant and subdominant), with their thirds and fifths, as in the following table.

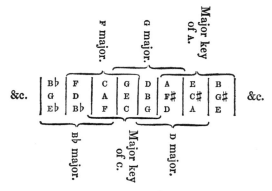

And so also in the minor keys, as in the following table.

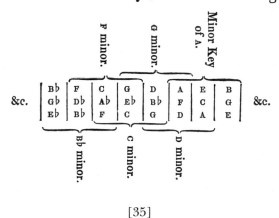

But as the very same notes are repeated in the above table, the following is preferable, in which the horizontal mark — signifies a fifth; the perpendicular | or oblique ╱, signifies a major third; and the dotted line ⋮ or ⟍., a minor third.

```
Bb— F — C — G — D — A — E — B —F♯—C♯—G♯—D♯—A♯—E♯—B♯— F♯♯, &c.
 | ⟍ | ⟍ | ⟍ | ⟍ | ⟍ | ⟍ | ⟍ | ⟍ | ⟍ | ⟍ | ⟍ | ⟍ | ⟍ | ⟍ | ╱ | ⟍
Gb—Db—Ab—Eb—Bb— F — C — G — D — A — E — B —F♯—C♯—G♯—D♯—A♯
 ⋮╱⋮╱⋮╱⋮╱⋮╱⋮╱⋮╱⋮╱⋮╱⋮╱⋮╱⋮╱⋮╱⋮╱⋮╱⋮╱
Bbb—Fb—Cb—Gb—Db—Ab—Eb—Bb— F — C — G — D — A — E — B — F♯
```

The middle row consists of key notes, excepting the first note and the last two notes, the upper row of major thirds to those notes, and the lower of minor thirds to them.   Thus a major triad is any note with its major third

and fifth, as
```
     E
     | ⟍
     c—G
```
in which E is major third to C, G is the fifth, and from E to G is a minor third; and a minor triad is thus expressed
```
      c—G
      ⋮╱
      Eb
```
a major key consists of three major triads, as for instance that of C major

thus
```
     A — E — B
     | ⟍ | ⟍ | ⟍
     F— C — G —D
```
and a minor key consists of three minor triads, as for instance that of A minor, thus
```
      D — A — E — B
      ⋮╱⋮╱⋮╱
      F — C — G
```
a minor key consists occasionally of both minor and major triads, as
```
      F♯—C♯—G♯
      | ⟍ | ⟍ | ⟍
      D — A — E — B *
      ⋮╱⋮╱⋮╱
      F — C — G
```

* The triad of *Sol* in the minor key is frequently made a major triad.   See Cadences. The triad of *Fa* is sometimes made a major triad, especially if followed by the major triad of *Sol*.   See Chromatic Successions.   The triad of *Do* is also occasionally made major. See Full Close.

and though the same letter is found in each of the three lines of the foregoing table page 14, (as c, in the upper line, the third to Ab, c, in the middle line, the key note, and c, in the lower line, the minor third to the key note A,) yet none of the notes contained in one line are the same as those contained in either of the others*, but differ from them in a slight degree, as the student will perceive when he comes to study tuning.

From the foregoing table it appears that in order to perform fourteen major and minor keys accurately in tune, forty-nine different notes should be contained in every octave, for twelve keys forty-three notes, &c. &c. *viz.* ten notes for one major and minor key, and three more notes for every additional key†.

* *Viz.* Supposing that the key note of every major and minor key is one sound common to both keys; that the note c is key note to both c major and c minor; A to A major and A minor, &c. Some theorists, however, construct the minor key on the sixth note of the relative major key: thus making the key note of A minor different from that of A major, but the same sound with A in the key of c major or F major.

† Here it may be allowed to teach the student how to know in what key any piece, or any part of a piece of music, is written. In melody alone, the key is known by its leading note; but where there is harmony, it is chiefly known by the triads. The former method is liable to many exceptions, and is very uncertain, but the latter is comparatively easy and clear.

In melody, (without harmony,) to find the leading note of a piece of music, or of any passage contained in any piece, let a table of leading notes standing a fifth from each other, be extended to any required length, as follows:

Bb   F C G D A E B F♯ C♯ G♯ D♯ A♯ E♯ B♯ F♯♯ C♯♯, &c.

Take the seven or more different notes of which the passage consists, and that note which stands latest in the foregoing table is the leading note of the key. Thus let it be required to know in what key the notes B D F G♯ A C E are, Example 17; by looking for them in the foregoing table, they will be found in the following order, F C D A E B G♯; G♯ therefore is the leading note, and as the key note is always one semitone higher than the leading note (See Note †, p. 7.) the key must be A, the third to A is c, and being a minor third, the key

[37]

Successions of triads are either diatonic or chromatic. Diatonic successions of triads are either simple or mixed.

Simple Diatonic Successions.

The three major triads of the major key, with the three minor triads of the relative minor key forming one diatonic scale on a keyed instrument, (page 14,) a succession of these in any order, and for any length of time is allowable; and when the order is regular, the succession is, in this work, called a simple diatonic succession of triads.

As some of these are become obsolete, and those still used are not all equally agreeable, it is necessary to treat of them separately.

They may be divided into such as move a fifth, a third, and a second; or

is A minor. In Example 18, the leading note is c♯, and the key D minor. In Example 19, the leading note is B♯, and the key c♯ minor. All the foregoing examples, however, are chromatic. Example 20 is diatonic, and may either be the key of c major (B being the leading note) or the ancient diatonic key of A minor without any leading note, the seventh, or subtonic, being a flat or minor seventh. (See Note ‡, p. 8.) But besides the difficulties which occur whenever the scale is diatonic, there are others owing to chromatic passages and ornamental notes, as in Example 21, which render this method very uncertain.

But in harmony wherever the triads are clearly distinguishable, (and, in this work, every combination will be derived from them,) the key will be easily known. Thus three major triads, standing a fifth from each other will constitute a major key; as the three, in Example 22, constitute the key of A major; and three minor triads, at a fifth from each other, form a diatonic minor key; as those in example 23, form the key of D minor.

In chromatic minor keys, when there is one minor triad and two major, the latter being a second from each other, the minor triad is that of *Do*; as in Example 24, where the key is E minor.

In example 25 is a series of triads in various keys. The triads bearing two names, as Sol in one key, and Do in another, are called doubtful chords; and will be explained hereafter.

[38]

their inversions, a fourth, a sixth, and a seventh. See page 6. There are six simple diatonic successions, *viz.*

> 1st, falling 5ths, or rising 4ths, which is the same thing *.
> 2nd, rising 5ths, or falling 4ths, ...
> 3rd, falling 3rds, or rising 6ths, ...
> 4th, rising 3rds, or falling 6ths, ...
> 5th, falling 2nds, or rising 7ths, ...
> 6th, rising 2nds, or falling 7ths, ...

First Simple Diatonic Succession : falling fifths or rising fourths. Any triad, except Fa, may fall a fifth, or rise a fourth; Fa cannot, because the fifth below, or the fourth above Fa, is the dissonant triad.

Thus the triad of *Sol* may be succeeded by that of	*Do*.		Example	26
. .	$\overline{Do}$	. . . .	$\overline{Fa}$,	. . 27
. .	$\overline{Fa}$ †	. . . .	$\overline{Sol}$,	. . 28
. .	$\overline{Sol}$	. . . .	Do,	. . 29
. .	Do	. . . .	Fa,	. . 30

Any two or more of these may be used together ; as in Example 31.

Some composers have introduced the dissonant triad into this succession only. Example 32. In which case it is considered as an inversion of $\underline{Fa}$ with a 6th. See added 6th.

Second Simple Diatonic Succession : rising fifths or falling fourths. Any triad, except $\underline{Sol}$, may rise a fifth, or fall a fourth; $\underline{Sol}$ cannot, because the fifth above, or fourth below $\underline{Sol}$, is the dissonant triad.

* The composer may rise 5ths or fall 4ths alternately, or when he pleases; and so of the rest.

† When *Fa* is succeeded by either of the triads of the major key, it is more properly considered as an inversion of Fa with a 6th in the major key. See Gradual Modulation, added Sixth &c., for the lowest note of a triad is not always the fundamental note.

c

Thus the triad of Fa may be succeeded by that of Do.　Example 33

	Do		. . . .	Sol,	. .	34
	Sol		. . . .	*Fa,*	. .	35
	Fa		. . . .	$\overline{Do,}$	. .	36
	$\overline{Do}$		. . . .	$\overline{Sol,}$	. .	37

Any two or more of these may be used together　.　.　.　38

Third Simple Diatonic Succession : falling thirds or rising sixths.　Any triad, except $\overline{Fa}$, may fall a third or rise a sixth; *Fa* cannot, because the third below, or sixth above, is the dissonant triad.

Thus the triad of Sol may be succeeded by that of $\overline{Sol}$.　Example 39

	$\overline{Sol}$		. . . .	$\overline{Do,}$	. .	40
	$\overline{Do}$		. . . .	$\underline{Do,}$	. .	41
	$\underline{Do}$		. . . .	$\overline{Fa,}$	. .	42
	$\overline{Fa}$		. . . .	$\underline{Fa,}$	. .	43

but the two first are peculiar to ancient music *.

Hence though any two or more of these examples *may* be used together; yet a combination of the three latter is, in general, to be preferred; especially in modern music.　Example 44†.

Fourth Simple Diatonic Succession : rising thirds or falling sixths. Any triad, except Sol, may rise a third or fall a sixth; Sol cannot, because the third above, or sixth below Sol, is the dissonant triad.

---

* By *ancient music* is meant that of the fifteenth, sixteenth, and seventeenth centuries. This is to be carefully distinguished by the student from *the music of the ancients*, *viz.* of the Greeks, Romans, and other ancient nations.

† The student may observe, that what he is cautioned to avoid in the *simple*, *may* be used with good effect in the *mixed* successions ; also, that what he is to avoid in the *modern*, is highly proper for the *ancient* style of music.　See his *Lectures on Music*.

Thus the triad of *Fa** may be succeeded by that of Fa.   Example 45

  ..   F̄a   ....   *Do,*   ..   46

  ..   *D̲o*   ....   D̄o,   ..   47

  ..   D̄o   ....   *Sol,*   ..   48

  ..   *S̲ol*   ....   S̄ol,   ..   49

But as these are all peculiar to ancient music the student is recommended to avoid them; unless he is writing professedly in the church style. Example 50.

Fifth Simple Diatonic Succession: falling seconds or rising sevenths. Any triad, except Do, may fall a second or rise a seventh; Do cannot, because the second below, or seventh above Do, is the dissonant triad.

Thus the triad of *D̲o* may be succeeded by that of Sol.   Example 51

  ..   S̄ol   ....   Fa †,   ..   52

  ..   Fa   ....   *Sol,*   ..   53

  ..   *S̲ol*   ....   *F̄a,*   ..   54

  ..   *F̲a* (or rather Fa)   D̄o,   ..   55

But the three latter examples are only fit for church music. Hence a combination of the two former is to be preferred to one of the three latter. Example 56.

Sixth Simple Diatonic Succession: rising seconds or falling sevenths. Any triad, except *D̲o,* may rise a second or fall a seventh; *D̲o* cannot, because the second above, or seventh below *D̲o,* is the dissonant triad.

Thus the triad of Do may be succeeded by that of *Fa.*   Example 57

  ..   *F̲a*   ....   S̄ol,   ..   58

  ..   S̲ol   ....   F̄a,   ..   59

---

* Or rather Fa with a 6th, inverted.   See Note, p. 21.

† The succession from Sol to Fa is by no means so common as from Sol to Do, or to D̲o.

                                             c 2

Thus the triad of Fa may be succeeded by that of Sol.   Example 60
        ..   Sol   ....   *Do*,   ..   61
The three former of these examples are only fit for the church style.
Hence a combination of the two latter is generally to be preferred to one of
the three former.   Example 62*.

Of the foregoing successions the first and second, Examples 31, 32, and
38, are the most agreeable to the ear; and should be most frequently used.
The next to be preferred is part of the third succession, as in Example 44;
then part of the sixth, Example 62; and lastly, part of the fifth, as in
Example 56.

Mixed Diatonic Successions.

The different ways of combining or mixing these simple diatonic
successions are very numerous.

The five following mixed successions are selected from these, and may be
denominated Mixed Diatonic Successions.

First Mixed Diatonic Succession: falling thirds and fifths alternately, or
rising sixths and fourths.   Thus the triads of *Sol*, Do, Fa, *Fa* (or rather
Fa, see note*, page 21) Sol, *Sol*, *Do*, Fa may succeed each other, Example
63, but the first note *Sol* is generally omitted†.

Second Mixed Diatonic Succession: rising thirds and fifths alternately,

* From *Fa* to *Sol*, and from *Sol* to Fa, is a good succession. See Chromatic successions.

† This succession is sometimes extended and rendered endless, by adding the dissonant
triad and that of Sol to it.   The dissonant triad, if followed by a chord in the minor key, is
derived from *Fa*, with a 6th (see added 6th), and when followed by one in the major key,
it is derived from the discord of Sol.   See Dominant 7th.

[42]

or falling sixths and fourths. Thus the triads of Fa, _Do_, _Sol_, Sol, _Fa_ (or Fa) Fa, Do, _Sol_, may succeed each other, Example 64 ; but the three first notes are less agreeable than the next four, Example 65, and the last note _Sol_ is generally omitted*.

Third Mixed Diatonic Succession : falling fifths and seconds alternately, or rising fourths and sevenths alternately. Thus the triad of _do_, _fa_, (or rather fa) do, fa, _sol_, _do_, sol, do, may succeed each other. Example 67.

Fourth Mixed Diatonic Succession : rising fifths and seconds alternately, or falling fourths and sevenths alternately. Thus the triads of Do, Sol, _Do_, _Sol_, Fa, Do, _Fa_, _Do_, may succeed each other. Example 68.

Fifth Mixed Diatonic Succession : rising seconds and falling thirds alternately, or falling sevenths and rising sixths alternately. Thus the triads of Sol, _Do_, Fa, Sol, _Sol_, Fa, _Fa_, _Sol_, Do, _Fa_, may succeed each other. Example 69.

Chromatic Successions.

A Chromatic Succession implies an alteration of the triads, from minor to major, in the minor key, occasioned by the occasional alterations of the 6th, 7th, and 3rd notes of the minor key, page 9.

Thus the triad of _Sol_ is frequently made major before or after the minor triad of _Do_, as in the first simple succession : see Examples 70, 71; the scale of which is thus rendered chromatic : in the second simple succession,

---

* The bass notes of this succession are often found in music, but not accompanied with a fifth and third to each note, the note _Sol_ having a sixth and third to it, which is an inversion of the triad of Do ; it becomes therefore, in this case, an irregular mixed diatonic succession. See Example 66.

Example 72; in the first mixed succession, Example 73; in the second mixed succession, Example 74; in the third mixed succession, Example 75; and in the fourth mixed succession, Example 76.

The dissonant triad, when used in the first simple diatonic succession, is derived from *Fa* with a sixth, inverted as *Re* with a third and a fifth. See p. 17, Example 32*. The third to *Fa* is often major in a minor key, p. 14, and Example 24. Thus *Fa* with a sharp third and sixth, when inverted, becomes *Re* with a third and sharpened fifth, as in Examples 77, 79, 80, where it is marked *Fa*. Example 77 is the first succession, but the transition from Fa to *Fa* is not agreeable. See added 6th.

Fa may have a major third in the second succession. Example 78. The first mixed succession may be used in the minor key by using *Re* with a sharpened 5th and minor 3rd, as the inversion of *Fa* with a sharp 3rd and 6th, as in Example 79: the transition, however, is not pleasing. It is better to use the major triad of *Fa*, as in Example 80. The major triad of *Fa* may be used in the second mixed succession. Example 81.

The triad of *Do* is sometimes major, especially after *Fa*, as in Ex. 82, and in Cadences; in this example the triad of *Sol* may be either major or minor.

Accompaniment.

In the foregoing successions, the fundamental notes only have been written, the accompaniment, or third and fifth to each bass note being only expressed by figures, which is called the thorough bass. For the manner of writing and performing this accompaniment, both in parts and on a keyed

---

* See inversions of the triad at the conclusion of the present chapter; see also **Discord of Fa** in the third chapter.

instrument, I shall now give rules, which will not only apply to successions triads, but to every other part of composition*.

Rule 1st†. Two‡ consecutive perfect§ fifths must not take place between the same parts ‖.

* Several composers (generally however from oversight) have left violations of these rules in their works. Dominico Scarlatti was perhaps the only one who professedly disregarded them for the sake of producing good effects. But whatever may have been the success of this great master, the passages, in which he has transgressed the rules, do not appear to have become the objects of imitation to other composers.

The method of accompanying the Chants of the Christian Church, by a succession of fifths, octaves, or fourths, used in and before the eleventh century, called Organum, (See Specimens, vol. ii. p. 1,) has been supposed to be the origin of harmony. The organ took its name from it; and the stops called cornet, sexquialtera, twelfth, tierce, principal, fifteenth, &c. are thought to have been invented to facilitate the performance of this accompaniment. But if the effect of this accompaniment was similar to that of the above stops of an organ, if, by being performed comparatively soft, it only enriched the tone without disturbing the melody, then it should not be considered as the origin of harmony, having no more to do with it than the harmonics which constantly accompany the melody of a single voice or instrument. The invention of harmony may be said rather to have commenced when these fifths, fourths, and octaves begun to be *avoided*.

† This rule is the most strict of any in music. The designed violations of it very rarely occur; they are sometimes met with in old madrigals by contrary motion (Example 88); but, having been exploded by modern composers, the rule should be most strictly adhered to by the student.

‡ (Page 28.) The repetition of the same notes in fifths, (Example 83,) is not considered as a violation of this rule; also if one part moves in octaves, while the other repeats the same note, (Example 84,) the rule is not violated: but if both parts move in octaves at once, remaining a fifth to each other, the rule is broken. Example 85.

§ (Page 28.) A perfect fifth may follow or be followed by an imperfect one, Example 86; not however between the treble and bass parts, but between the treble and some of the inner parts (see the following note.) Ex. 87. No other succession of a perfect and imperfect 5th being allowable.

‖ (Page 28.) By *parts* is meant the several melodies which, when combined, constitute

Thus, for instance, in a succession of any two chords, the part which is fifth to any other part in the one chord, must not be fifth to the same part in the next chord. Thus if the treble is fifth to the bass in one chord, it must be eighth or third, and not fifth, in the next; or, if the treble is fifth to the inner part, or the inner part fifth to the bass, or one inner part fifth to another, the same rule is to be observed. For examples of violations of this rule,

Between the treble and bass, . See Examples 88, 89.
.. the treble and inner parts, .. 90, 91.
.. one inner part and another, .. 92, 93.
.. the inner parts and the bass, .. 94, 95.

Rule 2nd*. Two† consecutive octaves, or unisons, must not take place between the same parts.

harmony: thus we speak of the violin, oboe, tenor, or other parts in a score, and of the treble, bass, upper, lower, or inner parts in music for keyed instruments. Students are recommended to write their tasks as much as possible in score, as the motion of the parts in music, adapted for keyed instruments, is not always easy to be discerned.

* This rule is the next in point of strictness to the foregoing. The violations of it by contrary motion occur more frequently than those of the former rule, Examples 101, 102, &c. &c. and may be allowed on pressing occasions, as in canons, fugues, &c. where the subject could not otherwise be preserved. This manner of evading the rule is generally allowed in music of more than four parts, though it should never take place between the upper and lower parts, but generally between the bass and one of the inner parts. The student is, however, recommended to keep the rule as strictly as possible.

† A repetition of the same notes in octaves is not against rule (Example 96). If one part moves while the other stands still, the rule is not broken (Example 97). But it is contrary to rule for both parts to move (Example 28); unless, indeed, the entire passage consists of octaves, and then a whole orchestra may perform in octaves to each other, and not break the rule (Example 99); and the word tasto, or tasto solo, expresses this absence of chords in the thorough bass.

[46]

Thus, for instance, in a succession of any two chords, the part which is octave to any other part in the one chord, must not be octave to the same part in the next chord. For examples of violations of this rule,

Method of accompanying the Triads in Thorough Bass.

In thorough bass it is usual to accompany each bass note in a succession of triads, with three notes in the right hand, the third, the fifth, and the eighth; the last of which is added for the sake of enriching the harmony. The position of these notes, and their distance from the bass note (especially from the first bass note) being arbitrary. Thus the triad of c may be accompanied in the right hand by the notes c, e, and g, at any distance from the bass note; as in Example 109: and thus the triad of f may be accompanied by f, a, and c, as in Example 110; and the triad of g, by g, b, and d, Example 111; but in the first chord of each of these examples the hands are too near each other; and, in the last, too far apart, for general purposes.

In modern music also, where the accompaniment consists of a number of essential notes (see Melody) in the way called arpeggio, octaves are allowable; but are not productive of any good effect, and should therefore be avoided. Example 100.

5ths and 8ves should not take place on the strongly accented or principal notes of the bar, though other notes may intervene. See page 31.

5ths and 8ves must not take place between two notes not struck together followed by two which are. The author has not directed his pupils to avoid what are called hidden 5ths and 8ves, as he finds no composers observe these rules since the period or writing plain counterpoint in only two parts.

In accompanying a succession of triads, the only rules which need be strictly observed are the two already given. But as there are various methods (some of which are more agreeable than others) of accompanying each succession, without the violation of the above rules, the following subordinate rules are offered to the student, to assist him in his choice.

First Subord. Rule. To make the upper part stand still, if possible; or, if not, to make it move by the smallest interval. Thus the accompaniments used in Example 112, though not against the rules of harmony, are far less agreeable than those in 113.

Second Subord. Rule. When the upper part cannot stand still, to make it move in a contrary direction to the bass, when that moves by the interval of a fifth, third, and second. Thus the accompaniment in Example 114, is not so agreeable as that in 115: hence the following rule*.

Third Subord. Rule. When the upper melody cannot stand still, to make it move in a similar direction to the bass, when that moves by the interval of a fourth, sixth, and seventh. Thus the accompaniment in Example 116, is not so agreeable as that in 117.

Fourth Subord. Rule. When the leading note is contained in one triad, and the key-note in the next, to have these two notes in the same part. Thus the accompaniments in Example 118, are less agreeable than those in 119.

Fifth Subord. Rule. In choosing the position of the first chord of the right hand at the commencement of a succession, regard must be had to the motion of the bass, so that the hands may not presently become too near, or

---

* This rule only relates to triads not inverted; see inversions of the triad. Some authors have extended the rule of contrary motion improperly to all motions of the bass, to avoid hidden 5ths and 8ves, concerning which the author gives no rules, considering them as obsolete.

too far apart. Thus in the first simple diatonic succession, as the base falls fifths or rises fourths, the accompaniment will rise, consequently the hands should be near each other at its commencement, and so also in the third and fifth simple diatonic successions. But in the second, fourth, and sixth simple diatonic successions, as the accompaniment will necessarily fall in contrary motion to the bass, the hands should not be near each other at the commencement.

Sixth Subord. Rule. Not to omit the third note of the triad, as in Example 120 *.

Seventh Subord. Rule. Not to double the third note of the triad, as in Example 121.

The latter rules are of less importance than the former.

The pupil should now, by way of exercise, transpose the bass notes of the successions of the triads into other keys, and play the accompaniment without its being written down.

Inversions of the Triad.

When the fundamental note of the triad † is in the bass, or lowest part, the harmony is direct; but when any other note is in the bass, the harmony is inverted.

There are two inversions of the triad:

1st. When the third note of the triad is in the bass, accompanied with a third and sixth. Example 122.

---

* In the last chord of a movement, ending in the minor key, the third was sometimes omitted by Handel and his cotemporaries.

† See note †, page 17.

2nd. When the fifth note of the triad is in the bass, accompanied with a fourth and sixth.   Example 123.

		5		6		6
		3		3		4
Thus the inversions of		Do	are	Mi	and	Sol,
		5		6		6
		3		3		4
. . . .		Fa	..	La	..	Do,
		5		6		6
		3		3		4
. . . .		Sol	..	Si	..	Re.

In accompanying these (whether in writing music, or in playing thorough bass) the sixth and seventh subordinate rules (page 27) should be generally adopted.   Thus, the third note of the triad should not be omitted, as in Example 124, nor doubled, as in Example 125.   If two notes are sufficient, the sixth and the third will be the best, but if more than two are wanted in the accompaniment, some other note may be doubled, as in Example 126, remembering always, however, that subordinate rules must give way to the two principal rules of avoiding perfect fifths and octaves.

The student, when composing music, may use either of these inversions in the middle of a passage*, for the sake of varying the bass.   Thus the chords in Example 127 may be varied, as in Examples 128 and 129.   The sixth and third may also be occasionally used on the first note of a passage,

---

* A passage in music is equivalent to a sentence in grammar; as the latter signifies an assemblage of words forming a complete sense, and consequently terminated by some sort of period, so the former means an assemblage of notes, which may be played by themselves, and are terminated by some sort of cadence.   See page 31.   The word is, however, often applied improperly to a combination of passages containing many cadences, but distinguishable from the rest of the piece by some peculiarity of rhythm, modulation, or expression, as when we speak of a quick passage, a loud passage, a chromatic passage, &c.

as in Example 130. But a passage must never begin with the sixth and fourth. A passage should seldom terminate with the sixth and third, and never with the sixth and fourth.

The sixth and fourth should be used very sparingly; and perhaps only in the two following ways: either when the triad from which it is derived is used before or after it, Example 131, or when it is followed by a fifth and third on the same bass note, especially on a pedale (Example 132). The sixth and fourth is indeed sometimes used on unaccented notes, as in Examples 133 and 134. The sixth and fourth on the 2nd note of the key in the bass (or the triad of Sol inverted as a $\frac{6}{4}$) is avoided by all good composers.

The student should be careful to use these inversions in such a manner only as can be supported by the authority of the best masters.

The chords of the sixth and third, and sixth and fourth, are not always inversions of a triad.

Thus the sixth and third on Fa is not an inversion of any triad, but is derived from the discord of a sixth fifth and third on Fa; see added Sixth. The sixth and third on Re is derived from the discord of a seventh fifth and third on Sol; see Dominant Seventh.

In the species of faburden *, called in this work a Succession of Sixes, the bass may ascend or descend throughout the octave, in the major key, every

* The succession of sixes and the pedale or drone bass (see discords of suspension and transition) are the only remains of a species of harmony called by the Italians, Falso Bordone, by the French, Faux Bourdon, and by the English, Faburden; in which each bass note had the same accompaniment, or in which every treble note was accompanied by the same bass note, like the drone of the bagpipe, and the bass of all pastorale movements. Haydn is, perhaps, the only one who has used the sixth and fourth on more than two bass notes, and that in only one place, Example 135; the author of this Treatise considers it as an inversion of the succession of sixes.

note being accompanied with a sixth and third, Example 136. Such a succession is not * considered as an inversion of triads.

In accompanying this succession, it will be found most convenient (in order to avoid consecutive perfect fifths and octaves) to have the sixth note in the upper melody. Example 136.

When more than two notes are required in the accompaniment, it will be necessary (in order to avoid consecutive perfect fifths and octaves) to double the third note of the triad in every alternate chord, as in Example 137 or 138, or the accompaniment may consist of two and three notes alternately. Examples 139 and 140; which may be written in parts, as in Examples 141 and 142.

When only the sixth and third on Re and Mi are used together (derived from Sol and Do, see Dominant Seventh) the third, instead of the sixth, may be in the upper melody, as in Examples 86 and 87; for the consecutive fifths in the accompaniment are not against rule, one of them being imperfect. When more than two notes are required in the accompaniment, they may be used as in Examples 143 and 144.

Detached parts of the succession of sixes are oftener found than the whole passage (Examples 137, 138, 139, 140, 141, and 142); and when the passage concludes with *Sol* in the minor key, the third note of the triad is made sharp (Examples 139, 140, 141, and 142). See Cadences.

* The sixth and fourth on Sol, when accented † and succeeded immediately

---

* If a succession of sixes were considered as an inversion of triads, then it would be allowable for a bass to ascend and descend through the octave, each note being fundamental (*viz.* accompanied with a fifth and third,) and including the dissonant triad; which is not the case. The first and last notes may, however, be considered as inversions and marked as such. See Example 136, where the first and last notes are called Do.

† See note *, next page.

by the fifth and third on the same note, is not, as it appears to be, the triad of Do inverted, but merely a double appoggiatura on the triad of Sol, and both chords are consequently considered as Sol; sometimes this chord is written in small notes, Example 145, but more frequently uniform characters. Examples 146, 147, 148, and 149.

The sixth and fourth oñ La (if ever used) is not an inversion of a triad, but is derived from the sixth, and third on Fa. See added Sixth.

The sixth and fourth on Fa is not an inversion of a consonant triad, but is derived from a seventh, fifth, and third on Sol (see Dominant Seventh); and as such sometimes succeeds the sixth and fourth on Sol; and both are then derived from Sol. Example 150.

Of Closes or Cadences.

A Close, or Cadence, is the termination, or last chord, of a passage*, which ought always to be an accented note†.

---

* The length of a passage is known by its close (p. 28, note*), and here a close is known by its being the end of a passage. In fact, there is often some difficulty in shewing which is the termination of a passage. In chants, the last chord of each part (*viz.* the note preceding each double bar) is the note of the cadence; or, in other words, the length of each passage is shewn by the double bars. Examples 148 and 149. In psalm tunes, by double bars; or, which is generally the same thing, by the length of the lines in the poetry. In recitative, by the length of the sentences. In instrumental music, it is generally at the end of every two or four bars. The last note of one passage is frequently the first note of the next.

† Of equal notes in common time, the first, third, fifth, and seventh are accented; the second, fourth, sixth, and eighth are unaccented. In triple time and triplets, the first of every three equal notes is accented; and the second and third unaccented. See Examples 151, 152, 153, 154, and 155. But in common time, the most accented notes (and on one of which the cadence should fall) are those which begin the bar, and the second half of the

There are four kinds of Cadence.

1st. When a passage ends with the triad of Do, that termination is called a full close, or perfect cadence, and is generally preceded by the triad of Sol, Example 162, *viz.* Sol Do in the major key, and $\overset{\sharp}{Sol}$ $\underline{Do}$ in the minor key. *In all Cadences* the triad of *Sol* in the minor key is to be a major triad. Sometimes also the triad of $\overline{Do}$ in the minor key is made a major triad after $\overset{\sharp}{Sol}$, Example 163, and vol. ii. Specimens, No. 4, page 1; and bar 6 of No. 11, page 5.

The sixth and third is sometimes used as an inversion of either Sol or Do in a full close, but very seldom however, and never at the conclusion of a movement. Example 164.

The fourth subordinate rule must be observed in this Cadence; *viz.* the leading note should be succeeded by the key note in the same part. The full close on Do may likewise be preceded by the dominant seventh; see

bar; or, in other words, a close should always fall on the beginning, or the middle of the bar: the first of these is preferable, though many instances might be adduced, from high authorities, of cadences falling on other notes; and even of the same cadence, in the same composition, falling on different parts of the bar. Example 156 is part of an air by Wagenseil, in which the close falls on the middle of the bar. Example 157 is the same air as written by Handel in his fifth harpsichord lesson, in which the cadence falls on the first note of the bar. Example 158 is part of a gavot, by Corelli, in which the cadence falls on the middle of the bar. Example 159 is a gavot in which the same master has placed all the cadences on the first note of the bar. Example 160 is a part of the celebrated Gloria in excelcis, by Pergolesi, in which the cadences are sometimes in the beginning and sometimes in the middle of the bar. Example 161 from the same composition, is an instance of a succession of cadences all falling on the middle of the bar, and which would certainly agree better with the established manner of beating time, were they placed at the beginning of each bar; in which case, the hand or foot, instead of being lifted at the conclusion of the passage, would fall when the last chord is struck.

Dominant Seventh: or it may be preceded by the triad of Fa, *viz.* Fa Do in the major key, and *Fa Do* in the minor key. Example 165.

Do* in the minor key is generally made a major triad after *Fa*, Example 166, and vol. ii. Specimens; No. 11, page 5, last bar.

The sixth and third is sometimes, though rarely, used as an inversion in this cadence, Example 167; and never at the conclusion of a movement.

The sixth and fourth on Do may be occasionally used as an inversion of Fa before Do, at a full close in church music, both in the major and minor keys, particularly at the end of a movement.

2nd. When a passage ends with the triad of Sol, that termination is called a half close, or imperfect cadence, and may be preceded by Do, Example 168 : *viz.* Do Sol in the major key, and *Do Sol* in the minor key.

The sixth and third is sometimes used in this cadence.

The sixth and fourth is sometimes used as an inversion of Do before Sol in this cadence, but never as an inversion of Sol.

The triad of Sol may likewise be preceded by that of Fa; Example 169; *viz.* Fa Sol in the major key, and *Fa Sol* in the minor key.

The sixth and third is sometimes used in this cadence as an inversion of Fa before Sol, but not of Sol; nor is a sixth and fourth used.

The half close never concludes a movement, unless another movement immediately succeeds.

3rd. When a passage ends with the triad of Fa, that termination is called a deceptive close, or deceptive cadence, and may be preceded by Do: *viz.* Do Fa in the major key, and *Do Fa* in the minor key; Example 170.

The sixth and third, and sixth and fourth, may be used in this cadence, as in the Example.

* This major triad of *Do* in the minor key was called the Tierce de Picardie, from having been invented, or much used, in that province.

D

The triad of Fa may be preceded by that of Sol, Example 171 ; but in this case the chord of Fa is generally inverted as a sixth and third. Example 172.

No other inversions are used in this cadence.

A movement never concludes with the deceptive close.

4th.   When a passage concludes with _Do_ in the minor key, preceded by either of the triads of the major key, (generally Sol,) or concludes with Fa in the major key, preceded by either of the triads of the minor key, (generally _Sol_,) that termination is called, in this work, a close delayed ; in other works, a false, flying, or abrupt cadence ; Example 173.   The only inversion in this cadence is that of Sol in the major key ; Example 174.

A movement never concludes with the close delayed.

The full close is the most frequently used ; next to that, the half close. The deceptive close and close delayed rarely occur.   Other terminations of passages may be met with in modern music, but they may be considered as licences till they become more generally adopted ; such as passages ending with discords, which can hardly be considered as regular cadences, nor can they easily be reduced to rule, as they are generally intended to produce surprise by their novelty.

✲ These marks (−) & (=) placed over the bass signify that the same chord is to be continued in the accompaniment.

✻ $\frac{4}{2}$ often stands for $\frac{6}{2}$ & the 6ᵗʰ. is, according to most writers to be supplied by the perfor_
mer of Thoro' Bass, only however when the Bass note falls one note in its resolution — if it
is succeeded by $\frac{5}{3}$ on the same bass note $\frac{4}{2}$ must not have a 6ᵗʰ added. The unexperienced
performer in thoro' bass is therefore recommended by the author of this work not to supply
the 6ᵗʰ. where it is omitted in the thoro' bass.

Ex: 257

The 4th understood.

✳ 4 3 stands for $\frac{5}{4}$ $\overline{3}$ or for $\frac{8}{5}$ $\overline{\overline{3}}$

Ex: 264.

Ex: 265. Ex: 266.

Ex: 267.

✳ 76 stands $\frac{76}{3}$ ✳98 stands for $\frac{98}{3}$

Ex: 289.

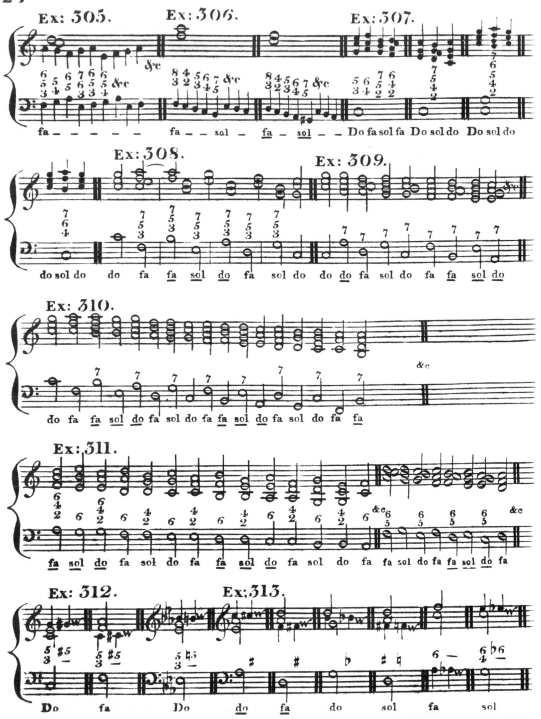

Chapter III.

OF DISCORDS.

A DISCORD is any combination of notes differing from a Concord, (see page 11,) and may consequently be known either by there being two notes next to each other, as to their alphabetical order, or some extreme flat or sharp interval.

Example 175 is a discord, because G and F are next to each other in the scale. Example 176 is a discord, though no two notes are together, because B and F form an extreme sharp fourth, or extreme flat fifth. Example 177 is a discord, because F and D♯ form an extreme sharp interval*.

When two notes, standing next to each other in alphabetical order, are struck together, the lowest of the two, according to that order, is called the discordant note. Thus in Example 175, in each of the chords, F is the discordant note; though it is sometimes in the upper part and sometimes in the lower part of the chord, sometimes over and sometimes under G; but it is the lowest when F and G are next to each other. In Example 178, D is

---

* When there is an imperfect interval, but no two notes next to each other in alphabetical order, some note is generally understood which would be next to another, if inserted.

Thus in the major key $\begin{smallmatrix}F\\D\\B\end{smallmatrix}$ are part of the discord of $\begin{smallmatrix}F\\D\\B\end{smallmatrix}$; and in the minor key $\begin{smallmatrix}F\\D\\G\end{smallmatrix}$ is part of the discord $\begin{smallmatrix}B\\A\\F\\D\end{smallmatrix}$ in which there are notes next to each other in alphabetical order.

D 2

the discordant note in each of the chords, because undermost, when D and E are struck together next to each other in the scale.

The discordant note should not be doubled or put in two of the parts.

A discord is resolved by the discordant note falling to the next note below, in the following chord or discord. Example 179. But before a discord is resolved, some of its notes may change places. Example 390, 439, 440, particularly 180 and 181.

Discords may be diatonic or chromatic.

By diatonic discords is meant, in this work, such as belong to the major key, including such chromatic discords as are mere transpositions of the same, from the major to the minor key, which is generally chromatic in modern music.

Diatonic discords are of four kinds; discords of addition, of suspension, of transition, and of syncopation.

I. *Discords of Addition.*

Discords of addition are so called because the note which occasions the discord may be added to the triad from which it is derived, when the composer pleases. They may be either on the accented or unaccented parts of the bar.

There are three discords of addition.

1st. The added seventh, discord of Sol, or dominant seventh. 2nd. The added sixth, great sixth, discord of Fa, or sub-dominant sixth. 3rd. The added ninth, or double discord of Sol, together with the leading seventh, which is derived from it.

1st. The added seventh, discord of Sol, or dominant seventh, is a seventh, added to the triad of Sol, (the dominant,) or is a seventh, fifth, and third upon Sol, the third being major, whether in the major or minor key.

[78]

In resolving this discord, the seventh is the discordant note, and must therefore fall to the note below in the next chord or discord; page 35.

Thus, for instance, in the major key of c, the dominant seventh is $\begin{smallmatrix} F \\ D \\ B \\ G \end{smallmatrix}$ and the discordant note F must fall to E; but the only chord in the key of c which contains an E is the triad of Do $\begin{smallmatrix} G \\ E \\ C \end{smallmatrix}$. Therefore the usual resolution of the dominant seventh is into the triad of Do. And the rules to be observed are :—

1st.   The discordant note must fall : *viz.*   .   Fa to Mi

2nd.   The leading note must rise, that it may go to the nearest note   .   .   .   Si to Do

3rd.   Re may go to Do, that it may avoid consecutive fifths to the bass, and avoid doubling the third   .   .   .   Re to Do*

4th.   Sol, if in the bass, should either fall to Do, or stand still ; if it went to Mi it would double the third. When in the accompaniment, Sol should remain still   .   .   Sol   Do
or Sol   Sol

See Examples 182, 183, 184.

Example 185 shows the various resolutions of the dominant seventh, according to the above rules in a score of five parts, the fundamental note

---

* Re may go to Sol if it does not make fifths to the bass—as when that is Sol Sol ; but that never takes place in a cadence or conclusion of a movement : Re may also go to Sol in the accompaniment when Fa Mi is the bass.

of the dominant seventh being doubled; or, in other words, the discord consisting of an eighth, seventh, fifth, and third.

Example 186 is the resolution of the same discord in four parts, without the eighth, which occasions the omission of the fifth in the triad of Do.

Example 187 is another method in four parts, the discord consisting of an eighth, seventh, and third; the fifth being omitted.

Example 188 is another method in four parts, the discord consisting of an eighth, seventh, and fifth; the third being omitted. This method may be used for the sake of variety, but is not so agreeable as the former. See Sixth Subord. Rule, page 27.

Example 189 shows the resolution, in three parts, the discord being the seventh and third; the fifth omitted.

Example 190 contains other methods less agreeable. See Sixth Subord. Rule, page 27.

Example 191 contains all the foregoing methods, written in thorough bass for a keyed instrument.

Example 192 contains part of the foregoing methods transposed into the relative minor key, from the study of which it will be easy to transpose all the rest into the same key, (which is here recommended to the student as an exercise;) as also into several other major and minor keys.

In all the above methods, the bass note, Sol, instead of falling a fifth to Do, may occasionally remain on Sol, and have a sixth and fourth.

The inversions of the dominant seventh, are the sixth, fifth, and third on Si; sixth, fourth, and third on Re; and sixth, fourth, and second on Fa. Example 193.

These are all resolved according to the foregoing rules, page 37.

For the resolution of the sixth, fifth, and third on Si, in four parts, see Example 194; for the same, in three parts, 195 and 196. In the latter

Example the fundamental note Sol is omitted, and the discord becomes the dissonant triad; the inversions of which will occur hereafter. In accompanying the dissonant triad it is best not to double the bass, or, in other words, to have no eighth.

Example 197 is a repetition of the same, written for keyed instruments.

Example 198 is in the relative minor key, into which the student should transpose the whole, as well as into other keys.

The resolutions of the sixth, fourth, and third on Re, are, in this work, only written for keyed instruments; and the student may write them in score, as well as transpose them.

The fundamental note Sol, as inserted in Example 199, is peculiar to modern music. Handel, Corelli, and other composers of the same period with them, avoided fourths to the bass note as much as possible, and wrote this discord as in Example 200: *viz.* as an inversion of the dissonant triad.

Example 201 shows how this discord is frequently used as part of the succession of sixes. If the third or discordant note is doubled, as in Example 200, the upper one falls and the lower rises.

Example 202 is used for the sake of a variety; the sixth note from the bass (*viz.* the third note from the fundamental note Sol) is omitted; contrary to the Sixth Subordinate Rule, page 27.

Example 203 shows this inversion in the minor key of A.

The resolutions of the sixth, fourth, and second on Fa are likewise in this work only written for keyed instruments; see Examples 204 and 208.

Either of the notes of the sixth, fourth, and second may be omitted in the accompaniment; Examples 205, 206, and 207. But the omission of the fourth (*viz.* of the third note from the fundamental note) has a bad effect, being contrary to the Sixth Subordinate Rule, page 27.

The dominant seventh and its inversions are sometimes irregularly

[81]

resolved into other chords, not in the same key, which contain a note to
which the discordant note may fall.

Thus the dominant seventh $\begin{smallmatrix}F\\D\\B\\G\end{smallmatrix}$ may be resolved into any chord or discord

which has an E to which the discordant note may fall, as

E	E	E	E	E	B♭
C	C♯	B	D	D	G
A	A	G♯	B	B	E
			G♯	G	C

See Example 209. And thus the dominant seventh in the minor key
$\begin{smallmatrix}D\\B\\G\sharp\\E\end{smallmatrix}$ may be irregularly resolved into $\begin{smallmatrix}C\\A\\F\end{smallmatrix}$ Example 210; but not into $\begin{smallmatrix}C\\G\\E\end{smallmatrix}$ because
the leading note G♯ must never fall one semitone, in this way, after the
dominant seventh, excepting in chromatic modulations, as Example 211.

2nd. The added sixth, great sixth, discord of Fa, or subdominant sixth,
is a sixth added to the triad of Fa, or is a sixth, fifth, and third upon Fa,
which is the root; Do, the fifth, being the discordant note. It may be preceded by either of the triads Do, Fa, or Sol, Example 212: or by a seventh,
fifth, and third on Fa; Example 213.

In resolving this discord, the discordant note must fall to the note below;

page 35. Thus, for instance, in the major key of C the added sixth is $\begin{smallmatrix}D\\C\\A\\F\end{smallmatrix}$

and the discordant note C must fall to B. But the only chord in the key of

C which contains a B, is the triad of Sol $\begin{smallmatrix}D\\B\\G\end{smallmatrix}$, or the discords of the dominant seventh $\begin{smallmatrix} F \\ D \\ B \\ G \end{smallmatrix}$; added ninth $\begin{smallmatrix} A \\ F \\ D \\ B \\ G \end{smallmatrix}$, or leading seventh $\begin{smallmatrix} A \\ F \\ D \\ B \end{smallmatrix}$; derived from it.

When this discord is resolved into the triad of Sol, the following rules should be observed.

1st.   The discordant note Do must fall to Si.

2ndly.   Re may remain on Re, or (especially if in the bass) go to Sol. It must do so when accompanied by a $\begin{smallmatrix} 7 \\ 5 \\ 3 \end{smallmatrix}$.

3rdly.   La may go to Sol to avoid doubling the third, or to Re, if it avoids fifths; but this is only in the accompaniment, never in the bass.

4thly.   Fa should generally go to Sol; see Examples 214 and 215.

Example 216 shows the resolution of this discord into the triad of Sol, in four parts, for keyed instruments.

Example 217, in three parts, with the third omitted, which has a better effect in this discord than in most others.

Example 218, in three parts, with the fifth omitted.   This chord in the major key of C, consisting of the same notes $\begin{smallmatrix} D \\ A \\ F \end{smallmatrix}$ with the inverted triad of _Fa_ in the relative minoi key of A, $\begin{smallmatrix} A \\ F \\ D \end{smallmatrix}$ is only distinguishable from that by being succeeded by another chord in the same key*.   Thus the sixth and third on F in Example 218, and the sixth and third on F in Example 219, are alike, but that in Example 218 is known to be the sixth, fifth, and third

---

* Fa with a ♮ may be succeeded by the triad of either Sol or Do.

on Fa in the major key of c with the fifth omitted, by the succeeding chord of Sol in the same key; and that in Example 219 is known to be an inversion of *Fa* in the minor key of A, by the following chord of *Sol* in the same key.

Examples 220 and 221 are transpositions of Examples 216, 217, and 218 into the relative minor key. But the transition from La to Si, *viz.* from F to G♯, Example 221, (which was made that the third note of the triad of Sol might not be omitted; see Sixth Subord. Rule, page 27,) has a bad effect, being three semitones. Examples 222 and 223 contain a better method. The third of the discord of *Fa* in the minor key may be occasionally sharp, as Examples 224 and 225*.

The sixth and third on *Fa*, in the minor key, may be mistaken for the sixth and third, derived from the sixth fourth and third on Re in the major key, with the fourth omitted; Examples 200 and 201; but may be distinguished from it by the succeeding chord being in the same key. Thus in Examples 226 and 227, the first chords of each are a sixth and third on D; the first is known to be in the major key of c, by the succeeding chord Do; and the other is known to be in the minor key of A, by the succeeding chord *Sol.*

The $\frac{6}{3}$ on Fa, may also be followed by a $\frac{5}{4}$ or $\frac{6}{4}$ on Sol, whether in the major or minor key.

The inversions of the added sixth, are a sixth fourth and third on La, a sixth fourth and second on Do, and a seventh fifth and third on Re. Example 230.

---

* Though *La* in the minor key seldom ascends to *Si*, the leading note in the minor key, because the interval is three semitones, as already mentioned, yet it often descends to the leading note below, as in Example 228. On the contrary, though *La*♯ (the major third to *Fa*) often ascends to the leading note, Example 225, yet it never descends, as Example 229.

Example 231 shows the resolution of the sixth fourth and third, which is the least common inversion of the three. The third in this chord is never omitted, (for the sixth and fourth is seldom used, excepting on Do, Fa, and Sol;) and if the fourth is omitted it ceases to be a discord; the sixth, however, may be omitted. Example 232.

Example 233 is the sixth fourth and third in the minor key.

Example 234 is the resolution of the sixth fourth and second on Do: the fourth or the sixth may be omitted; but not the second, as it then ceases to be a discord. In this inversion Re might go to Sol, and Fa to Re.

Example 235 is the resolution of the seventh fifth and third on Re, with its occasional omissions of the fifth, the third, and the seventh. The fifth and third on Re resembles the chord of *Fa* in the minor key, and is distinguished from it by the following chord. Thus in Examples 236 and 237,

the triad of $\overset{\text{A}}{\underset{\text{D}}{\text{F}}}$ is alike in both, but the following chord in Example 236 determines the key to be c major; and in Example 237, the following chord determines the key to be A minor.

Example 238 is the same discord in the minor key. This may also be mistaken for the leading seventh in the key of c, and is distinguished in the same way, *viz.* by the following chord. Thus Example 238 is in the key of A minor, and Example 239 in the key of c major.

When the added sixth (or any of its inversions) is resolved into the dominant seventh, the discordant note Fa of the latter discord may succeed either Re, La, or Fa in the same part, but seldom, if ever, Do, because Do is the discordant note of the former discord, and must fall to the note below. See Example 240.

3rdly. The added ninth, or double discord of Sol, is a ninth added to the dominant seventh *. See Example 241. The third is always major, whether in the major or minor key.

The ninth is more frequently in the upper melody than either of the other notes.

La is the peculiar discordant note of this discord, and must fall to Sol. Fa, however, (the seventh,) is also a discordant note, and must fall to Mi, either at the same time, or immediately afterwards.

If La falls first, this discord is resolved into the dominant seventh. Example 242.

If La and Fa are resolved together, by both falling to the notes below at the same time, *viz.* La to Sol, and Fa to Mi, this discord is resolved into the triad of Do, either as a fifth and third, or as a sixth and fourth, which is preferable; but not as a sixth and third: Example 243.

The third note of this discord is seldom omitted, as in Example 244.

The fifth may be omitted, as in Example 245.

The seventh very seldom is omitted; Example 246.

The fifth and third may both be omitted; Example 247.

The ninth seventh fifth and third, when it has no omission, must not be inverted.

But the most usual and beautiful omission in this discord is that of the fundamental note, Sol. This discord then becomes a seventh fifth and third on Si, the leading note of the key; and hence it is called, in this work, the leading seventh. In the minor key it is sometimes called the diminished seventh, all its intervals being minor.

Its resolutions may be seen, Example 248; its omissions, Example 249.

It is sometimes inverted as a sixth fourth and third on Fa: Example 250. The third (which had been the ninth) being at the top.

* This discord is of modern invention, and not proper for church music.

[86]

The sixth of this latter discord may be omitted, Example 251, but not the fourth.

The $\frac{6}{3}$ on Re, the second note of the key, may also be used with the fifth at the top : in its use the bass must ascend to Mi with a sixth.

Other inversions of this discord may be met with in modern music in the minor, but not in the major key; Example 252.

II. Discords of Suspension.

Discords of suspension are so called because the discordant note must be suspended from a note, in the same part of the preceding chord or discord; and they are always accented*.

The principal discords of suspension are :

1st.   The $\frac{5}{4}$.

2nd.   The $\frac{9}{3}$.

3rd.   The $\frac{7}{3}$.

4th.   The $\frac{7}{3}$ on Fa.

5th.   Discords of addition prepared.

6th.   Discords of suspension on a pedale—and

7th.   Double discords.

1st.   The discord of a fifth and fourth is generally used on Sol, and frequently on Do; but seldom, if ever, on Fa in the major key, because the

---

* They are also called prepared discords, preparation signifying this existence of the discordant note in the preceding chord. Being accented notes they resemble appoggiaturas, and some authors have therefore called them suspended appoggiaturas; for they are sometimes written as ornamental notes, as in Example 253, and sometimes as part of the chord, Example 254.

fourth is extreme sharp*. It may be used on either _Do_, _Fa_, or _Sol_, in the minor key.

The fifth and fourth is resolved into the fifth and third, the fourth being the discordant note, which must fall to the note below, and must be prepared, or suspended from the preceding chord or discord; Example 255.

The only inversion of the fifth and fourth is the fifth and second; the other inversion of the seventh and fourth is never used on account of the fourth to the bass note, after its resolution.

The fifth and fourth on Sol in the major key may be prepared by the triads of Do, or of Fa, by the discord of Fa, and by the triad of _Do_ in the minor key, and their inversions.   Example 256.

The fifth and fourth on Do may be prepared by the triad of Fa, by the dominant seventh, and their inversions, by the triad of _Fa_, in the minor key, and by Fa with a sixth and third, Example 257; but not by the sixth fifth and third on Fa, which could not be resolved if succeeded by this discord.   For the fifth and fourth on Do, prepared by the triad of _Fa_ in the minor key, see Example 258, where it is written in parts, to show how the discord is prepared or suspended.

The fifth and fourth on _Do_ in the minor key, may be prepared by the triad of _Fa_ in the same key, or by the dominant seventh and their inversions, with the same inversions, omissions, &c., as were used in the major key.   Example 259.

The fifth and fourth on _Fa_ in the minor key is generally prepared by the triad of Sol in the major key.   Example 260.

The fifth and fourth on _Sol_ in the minor key may either be resolved into

* It is sometimes used as an _unprepared_ appoggiatura on Fa in modern music; and sometimes together with the ninth.

the major or minor triad of *Sol*; and may be prepared by the triad of *Do*, by the triad of *Fa*, by the discord of *Fa*, or sometimes by the triad of *Fa* in the major key, with their inversions, &c. Example 261. For the preparation of this discord by the triad of Fa in the major key, see Example 262.

The fifth and fourth on Sol may likewise be resolved into the dominant seventh, and may be accompanied by the dominant seventh, and sometimes with the added ninth. Example 263.

As a discord of transition it will likewise have different resolutions from the foregoing. See Discords of Transition.

The composer may vary the second simple diatonic succession by accompanying each bass note (excepting the first) with a $\frac{5}{43}$. Example 264.

This has given rise to a beautiful passage frequently occurring in ancient music, which will never become obsolete or uninteresting. Example 265.

2nd. The ninth fifth and third, may be used either on Do, Fa, or Sol, in the major or minor key; the third to *Sol* in the minor being generally major. This discord has no inversions unless there is an omission of the fundamental note.

The ninth is the discordant note, and must fall to the eighth *.

The ninth fifth and third on Do may be prepared by the triad of Sol, by Fa with a sixth and third, or by the dominant seventh, and such of their inversions as are contained in Example 266.

The ninth fifth and third on Fa is generally prepared by the triad of Do, or by that of *Sol* in the minor key; not often, if ever, by Sol in the major key, excepting as in the inversions. Example 267.

The ninth fifth and third on Sol is prepared by the triad of Fa, seldom

---

* The ninth must fall to the note below; but sometimes the bass falls a third at the same time, or rises a third.

by that of _Do_ in the minor key, excepting as in the inversions of the 9 8. Example 268.

The ninth fifth and third on _Do_ in the minor key may be prepared by the triad of Sol in the major key, by that of _Sol_ in the minor key, by _Fa_ in the minor key with a sixth and third, by the dominant seventh and some of its inversions, and by the leading seventh.   Example 269.

The ninth fifth and third on _Fa_ in the minor key, may be prepared by the triad of _Do_, by that of Do in the major key, or _Sol_ in the minor key, as used in Example 270.

The ninth fifth and third on _Sol_ is prepared by the triad of _Fa_ in the minor key, or by Fa, as in Example 271.

In the fourth mixed diatonic succession the fifth and fourth, and the ninth fifth and third may be alternately used, as in Example 272.

In the third mixed diatonic succession also, the fifth and fourth, and the ninth fifth and third, may be alternately used, as in Example 273, which is written in parts to show how the discords are prepared.

3rd.   The seventh and third (which has been considered as one of the omissions derived from the ninth fifth and third) may be used as a suspended discord on any note of the scale.   The seventh is the discordant note, and must fall to the sixth.

Thus the succession of sixes may be converted into a succession of these discords.   Example 274 *.

---

* When a fifth and third, succeeded by a sixth, appears on each note of an ascending bass, the author of the present work cannot help regarding the fifth as an unessential note, a sort of appoggiatura resolved irregularly upwards into the sixth, as the seventh was downwards. Example 275.

When, however, the first part only of the passage is used, it may be regarded, as it indeed is by most authors, as an inversion of the first mixed diatonic succession.   Examples 63 and 276.   But the latter part of the passage cannot be so derived.

[90]

This discord, being a prepared appoggiatura on a sixth and third, ought not, perhaps, to have any fifth; yet many instances may be found in the works of the best composers, where the fifth seems to be inserted merely for the sake of making the harmony fuller. The fifth is always omitted in the resolution.

Thus the half close, Example 277, is used by Corelli as in Example 278.

And thus Example 279 may be converted into Example 280. This, however, may be otherwise derived. Example 281.

The whole succession is sometimes so accompanied. Example 282.

The seventh and third, succeeded by a sixth, is sometimes inverted as a fourth and second, the bass note then being the discordant note. A succession of these may be found, but is not recommended.

4thly. The seventh, fifth, and third on Fa, is prepared either by the triad of Do in the major key, or of _Do_ in the minor key, and is resolved into the discord of Fa; the seventh, fifth, and third on _Fa_, is prepared either by the triad of _Do_, or of Fa, and is resolved into the discord of _Fa_. Examples 283 and 284.

This discord is sometimes used without preparation; sometimes irregularly resolved, and sometimes unaccented. Example 285.

It is sometimes preceded by the dominant seventh. Example 285.

It is sometimes resolved into the sixth and fourth on Sol, when it is generally unaccented.

When inverted, as a sixth and fifth, this discord is often resolved into the dominant seventh, inverted as a sixth and fifth. Example 286.

5th. Any of the discords of addition may be accented, prepared, and resolved, as discords of suspension. Example 287.

6th. Suspended discords may be used with a holding note in the bass,

E

called, in this work, the pedale : such are the seventh and sixth, sixth and fifth, fifth and fourth, fourth and third, ninth and third, ninth and eighth, and the eighth and seventh.

This pedale, or holding note in the bass, is generally Sol, sometimes Do, but seldom Fa. See Examples 288, 289, and 290.

The derivation of some of these is at present unintelligible to the student, as they come from the discords of transition.

The young composer is recommended to be sparing in the use of the pedale on Fa; and to be careful to have sufficient authority for any passage of the kind he uses.

The pedale * on Sol or Do may be used with all the discords of suspension, as well as those of transition, and, indeed, with almost every kind of passage whatever.

This causes an endless diversity of figures, and an apparent irregularity of resolution, which disappears if the student considers the passage without the pedale note.

For several discords of suspension on a pedale, see Example 291.

7th. Among discords of suspension are likewise placed all double discords, in which two or more notes are suspended and resolved together.

As the ninth and fourth, or ninth fifth and fourth.　　Example 292.
　.. ninth and seventh, or ninth seventh and third.　　.. 293.
　.. ninth seventh and fourth.　　.　　.　　.. 294.
　.. ninth seventh fifth and third.　　.　　.　.. 295.

---

* The pedale bass probably had its origin in the music composed for the bagpipe, the drone of which is still imitated in all pastoral music. It is a species of Faburden mentioned page 29.

As the seventh fifth fourth and second * on Do.   Example 296.

..   seventh fifth and fourth   .   on Sol.   . ..   297.

..   ninth seventh fifth and fourth   on Sol.   . ..   298.

And perhaps some others used occasionally by such composers as excel in intricate harmony.

III. *Discords of Transition.*

Discords of Transition are so called because the generality of them consist of passing notes †, combined with holding notes; and they are generally unaccented. The principal of these are :—

1st. The eighth, followed by the seventh, and its inversions; also the fifth, followed by the sixth; the third, by the fourth, &c.

2nd. Notes ascending or descending diatonically, with one or more holding notes in the other parts, as the fourth and second, and its inversions.

3rd. Discords of addition, on a pedale, not prepared, as the sixth fourth and second; seventh fifth fourth and second, &c.

1st. For the eighth, followed by a seventh and its inversions, see Example 299.

It may be used on each note of the scale, as in the first simple diatonic succession. Example 300.

Of this kind of discord also are the fifth, followed by a sixth ‡, and third

---

* The seventh fifth fourth and second, on Do is the dominant seventh, with a pedale bass on Do; Fa falls, but Si rises according to the rules already given for the resolution of the dominant seventh. It has been written $\frac{11}{\substack{9\\7\\5}}$ by some authors.

† Unessential notes, and passing notes, will be hereafter defined.

‡ The 6 after a 5, and the 4 after a 3, are not discordant notes, but rather unessential notes.

E 2

by a fourth, and all other similar processes wherein the latter note, though not discordant, is unessential, unaccented, and figured in the thorough bass. Example 301.

2nd.   Notes ascending or descending diatonically, with one or more holding notes in the other parts.   Example 302.

These produce a variety of figures, the principal of which are the fourth and second on Do, Fa, or Sol, and its inversions.   Example 303.

The chord of Do, or part of it sustained.   Example 304*.

The sixth and fifth to Fa sustained.   Example 305.

The eighth and third to Fa.   Example 306.

3rd.   Triads, sixes, and discords of addition, not suspended, may be used on a pedale.   Example 307.

IV.   *Discords of Syncopation.*

Discords of Syncopation are so called because in ancient music they were written in syncopated notes, *viz.*, notes beginning always on the unaccented part of the bar.   Example 308.   The discordant notes must always be prepared.

These are a seventh fifth and third, on each bass note, or on every alternate bass note, of the first simple diatonic succession.   For the seventh fifth and third on each bass note, see Example 309.   This passage is seldom, if ever, inverted.   For the seventh fifth and third, on alternate bass notes, see Example 310.   This passage admits of certain inversions. Example 311.

---

* Part of this example is in the key of Eb, and the key note is called Do; another part is in F.

Chromatic Harmonies.

Chromatic Harmonies are such as are peculiar to the chromatic scale, page 4, not including such chromatic discords as are mere transpositions of diatonic discords from the major into the minor key. They always occasion an alteration of flats and sharps without a change of key. The principal chromatic harmonies are :—

    1st. Chromatic passing notes.
    2nd. Certain discords of transition altered.
    3rd. The minor ninth to Sol and its omissions.
    4th. The discords of Fa sharp *.
    5th. The Italian, German, and French sixes.
    6th. The Neapolitan sixth.
    7th. The flat seventh to the key note.

    1st. Chromatic passing notes are numerous, as the extreme sharp fifth. Example 312. Minor thirds after major in the same key, or *vice versa*, and their inversions. Example 313. The octave sharpened, Example 314, and various others.

    2nd. The sharp fourth and sharp second are sometimes used as passing notes, and frequently (in modern music especially) used instead of the diatonic fourth and second, Example 315 † ; for its inversions, see Example 318. For other passages of a similar kind, see Example 319.

---

    * By Fa sharp is meant the half note above Fa. Thus, in the key of c major, Fa sharp is F♯ ; in the minor key of A, _Fa_ sharp is D♯. Amongst flats, Fa sharp will of course be a natural ; in the key of B♭ it is E♮.

    † J. C. Bach uses the fourth sharpened without sharpening the second. Example 316. The inversions of this passage are not uncommon. Example 317.

3rd.   For the minor ninth to Sol in the major key, and its omissions, see Example 320.

4th.   For Fa sharp, with its discords, see Examples 321 and 322.   This may be resolved either into the triad, or the sixth and fourth, on Sol.

In the minor key the third to *Fa* sharp must also be sharp, otherwise the third would be extreme flat.   Examples 322 and 323.

The flat seventh on Fa sharp in the major key, especially after the sixth and fifth on Fa, is often written as an extreme sharp sixth and fifth, but is then always resolved into a sixth and fourth on Sol.   Example 324.

5th.   The Italian, German, and French sixes * are extreme sharp, both in the major and minor key; and are inversions of the triad of Fa.   They are never inverted.

The Italian sixth is accompanied with a third, and is resolved either into the triad of Sol, or the sixth and fourth on Sol.   Example 325.

The German sixth is accompanied with a fifth and third, and is resolved only into Sol with a sixth and fourth.   Example 326.

The French sixth is accompanied with a fourth and third, and may be resolved into either the triad of Sol, or the sixth and fourth on Sol †.   Example 327.

6th.   The Neapolitan sixth is a minor third and a minor sixth, both in the major and minor keys, to Fa, and is very seldom inverted.   It is resolved into the triad of Sol, Example 328; into the sixth and fourth on Sol, Example 329; into the diminished seventh on Fa sharp, Example 330; or into the triad of Do, inverted as a sixth and third, Example 331.   It is

---

* These and the Neapolitan sixes are denominated after the nations which invented them, or most frequently used them.

† It has been asserted that this discord is only to be found in French treatises : the author of this work has however, seen it in a song by Hasse.

sometimes also succeeded by a fifth; and has been used on the key note, and followed by Fa sharp.

7th. Flat sevenths of the key are occasionally met with, which do not seem to change the key: such is the fifth fourth and flat third on Sol, used by Purcell and others*; and its inversions. Example 332.

It is doubted whether the flat seventh to the key note, used with a fifth and third very commonly in national and other music, ought to be considered a change of key; and whether the key is affected by the flat seventh, used frequently in the bass previous to a modulation. Example 333.

---

* In the works of Purcell, Dom°· Scarlatti, Haydn, Mozart, Rossini, and other inventive geniuses, discords may be found not mentioned in this work; the foregoing are, however, the principal of those commonly used.

Chapter IV.

OF MELODY.

MELODY is a succession of single notes; but in scientific music it is considered as forming the accompaniment, or else the bass, of some harmony either expressed or understood *.

Melody consists of essential and unessential notes.

1st. Essential notes are such as form a part of the harmony. They may be either written in plain or florid counterpoint †.

2nd. Unessential notes are such as form no part of the harmony, and are not figured in the thorough bass; they are, therefore, never used without essential notes, and, together with them, always constitute florid counterpoint. They are of four kinds :—

* A few melodies in national music have been found incapable of harmony; such as the first two bars of the second part of the Irish tune, called ' The Fair Haired Child.'—Specimens, vol. i. p. 35, No. 53.

† Counterpoint is another term for harmony, or the writing the points or heads of the notes counter, opposite, or rather under each other. Plain counterpoint is when the notes of the accompaniment are of the same length with those in the subject. Example 334. Florid counterpoint is where the length of the notes, in the different parts, is various. Example 335. The rules of counterpoint are not given in this work, as they seem to have become obsolete. The study of double counterpoint, or of making an accompaniment to a given subject, which may be used either below it, as a bass, or above it, is useful, especially in making fugues. In Example 453, the same accompaniment is used an 8ve. below the subject, and a 12th above it.

[98]

(a) This is an Enharmonic Modulation. The A♯ is used instead of B♭

The last 4 Bars of "My Genial spirits droop."   Samson

Ex: 390

Extract from the 2ᵈ part of "Return O GOD of Hosts."

Ex: 391

From Haydn's Creation.

Ex: 392.

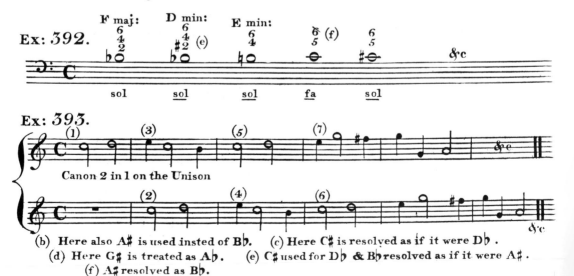

Ex: 393.

Canon 2 in 1 on the Unison

(b) Here also A♯ is used insted of B♭.   (c) Here C♯ is resolved as if it were D♭.
(d) Here G♯ is treated as A♭.   (e) C♯ used for D♭ & B♭ resolved as if it were A♯.
(f) A♯ resolved as B♭.

1st.   Passing notes.

2nd.   Appoggiaturas.

3rd.   Adjunct notes.

4th.   Notes of anticipation.

1st.   Passing notes are placed between one essential note and another, by a regularly ascending or descending melody.   They are generally unaccented, but sometimes accented.   When the essential notes are a fourth apart, two passing notes will sometimes succeed each other.   See Example 336, where each passing note is marked by a figure 1 placed over it.

Passing notes are occasionally chromatic, as in Example 337.

2nd.   Appoggiaturas are accented notes placed before essential notes, at the distance of one note either above or below them, Example 338, where each of the appoggiaturas is marked by a figure 2 over it.   In Example 339, the passing notes and appoggiaturas are marked as before.

Example 340 contains appoggiaturas placed below the essential note.

When appoggiaturas are placed below the essential notes they are frequently made chromatic by being raised one semitone, as in Example 341.

3rd.   Adjunct notes are unaccented, and placed before or after essential notes, one note above or below them.

In Example 342 the adjunct notes are marked by a figure 3.   They are frequently raised one semitone when placed below the essential notes. Example 343*.

4th.   Notes of anticipation are unaccented, following the essential notes, and belonging to the succeeding chord, Example 344, where they are marked by a figure 4.

---

* The author considers adjunct notes as the most difficult of any for the student to use correctly, or agreeably, unless he is guided by a very good ear and taste, and relies on the authority of good composers for the manner of adopting them.

Appoggiaturas and passing notes may be preceded by notes of anticipation, as in Example 345.

Sometimes two appoggiaturas will be found together. Example 346.

Passing notes, appoggiaturas, and notes of anticipation, are frequently expressed in little notes as well as large ones, or in different characters, as turns, inverted turns, and other graces. Examples 346 and 347.

Passing notes in melody differ from those in discords of transition only by not being figured in the thorough bass.

CHAPTER V.

OF MUSIC IN PARTS.

By Music in parts is here meant such as is intended for a number of voices, instruments, or both together, written in score, *viz.*, in separate lines one under another.

Music in parts may consist either, first, entirely of real parts; or, secondly, of real parts with others added, merely for the sake of effect.

The bass, or lowest part, should consist, generally, of the fundamental note, or of the third, but not of the fifth note of the chord *.

The same rules apply to the treble and bass, whether there are many, few, or no parts contained between them.

Glees, trios, quartetts, &c., are usually written in a score consisting of real parts.

2ndly. There are various ways of deviating from the strictness of real parts for the sake of effect; such as by a passage consisting entirely of unisons or octaves, or by one in which some of the parts are in octaves or unisons with each other, while the rest are distinct.

Anthems have a bass line for the organ, under the bass voice part, and chiefly in unison with it, to which are affixed the figures of the thorough bass. In symphonies, and other full instrumental music, the two violins

---

* A chord containing a fourth in the thorough bass, may, however, be occasionally used, provided the fourth is not expressed, but merely understood.

and the bass, or the two violins, viola, and bass, are real parts. In oratorio choruses, the voice parts are real; the vocal and instrumental basses are generally in unison when they perform together; and the two violins and viola form real parts when distinct from the voices. In songs, the violins, viola, voice, and bass, form real parts; or one of the violins may be in unison with the voice. The student will, however, be better able to acquire this kind of experience from the study of the works of good masters than from that of an elementary treatise.

Sometimes the bass is omitted entirely for the sake of effect; and the other parts remain the same as if it were retained. Example 348.

Tasks or Exercises for the Student.

The Student, having proceeded thus far, is recommended, 1st, to make scores of all the preceding Examples (not already written in parts) in as many lines as may be required.

2ndly. To harmonize, or make scores, of any simple composition, as a chant or psalm*, consisting only of a treble, or of a treble and bass; and these scores may consist of three, four, five, six, seven, or eight parts.

3rdly. To make a new harmony to a given bass, or inner part.

To perform either of these tasks, the student should be well acquainted with all the clefs in general use. Example 349.

4thly. To transpose all the foregoing examples into various keys.

5thly. The first attempt which the student should make at original composition may be preludes, or a series of chords, written without bars, and without any other change of key than that into the relative key already described, pages 19, &c.

* These tasks should be instrumental rather than vocal pieces.

6thly. The first attempt at music in time should consist merely of semibreves and minims, or of any other simple notes, care being taken that the suspended discords and the cadences are properly accented.

In order to do this, the student should be acquainted with every kind of time.

Of Rhythm or Time.*

Rhythm, or time, is of two kinds, common and triple. Common time contains two equal notes in each measure or bar, as two semibreves, two minims, two dotted minims, &c.

Triple time contains three equal notes in each measure, as three minims, three crotchets, three dotted crotchets, &c.

Common time is of two kinds, simple and compound.

In simple common time, the two equal notes of which the measure or bar consists, are not dotted, but are either semibreves, minims, or crotchets.

The time which has two semibreves is called *Alla Breve* time. See Example 350.

For that which has two minims, see Example 351.

Two crotchets are marked $\frac{2}{4}$, *viz.*, two fourths of a semibreve. Example 352.

In compound common time, the two equal notes are dotted, and are

---

* The author has thought it necessary to insert some things in this work with which the student ought, previously, to be thoroughly acquainted,—as the explanations of the clefs, and of the different sorts of time: he was induced to do so, from having observed that these particulars are not always taught, or if taught, are apt to be forgotten by the pupil, who, in other respects, may be enabled to understand the elements of musical composition and thorough bass.

either two dotted minims and six crotchets, two dotted minims and four dotted crotchets, or two dotted crotchets.

The time which has two dotted minims and six crotchets is marked $\frac{6}{4}$, *viz.*, six fourths of a semibreve, and is compounded of two bars of the time marked $\frac{3}{4}$. Examples 353 and 357.

That which has two dotted minims and four dotted crotchets, is marked $\frac{12}{8}$, *viz.*, twelve eighths of a semibreve, and is compounded of four bars of the time marked $\frac{3}{8}$. Examples 354 and 358.

That which has two dotted crotchets is marked $\frac{6}{8}$, *viz.*, six eighths of a semibreve, and is compounded of two bars of the time marked $\frac{3}{8}$. Examples 355 and 358.

Triple time is either simple or compound.

In simple triple time, the three notes of which the bar consists are not dotted, but are either minims, crotchets, or quavers.

The time which contains three minims in a bar is marked $\frac{3}{2}$, *viz.*, three notes, each equal to the half of a semibreve. Example 356.

That which has three crotchets is marked $\frac{3}{4}$, *viz.*, three fourths of a semibreve. Example 357.

That which has three quavers is marked $\frac{3}{8}$, *viz.*, three eighths of a semibreve. Example 358.

In compound triple time the three equal notes of which the bar consists, are either dotted minims, or dotted crotchets.

The time which has three dotted minims in a bar is marked $\frac{9}{4}$, *viz.*, nine fourths of a semibreve, and is compounded of three bars of the time marked $\frac{3}{4}$. Examples 359 and 357.

That which has three dotted crotchets is marked $\frac{9}{8}$, *viz.*, nine eighths of a semibreve, and is compounded of three bars of the time marked $\frac{3}{8}$. Examples 360 and 358.

Mixed measure is where a crotchet is divided into three quavers, or a minim into three crotchets, &c. Example 361.

The time called Alla Breve, and that marked $\frac{6}{4}$, $1\frac{2}{8}$, $\frac{3}{2}$, and $\frac{9}{4}$, is peculiar to ancient music; that marked $\frac{9}{8}$ is not common in modern music *.

---

* The student is supposed to be acquainted with the length of notes and rests, and all other such particulars, previous to his commencing composer; for unless he can read music well, and perform on a keyed instrument, the study of composition and thorough bass will be unattainable.

Chapter VI.

OF MODULATION.

MODULATION signifies a change of mode or key. Modulation is of three kinds—diatonic, chromatic, and enharmonic.

1st. For diatonic modulation, see the simple and mixed diatonic successions of the triads, page 17, &c.

2nd. Chromatic modulation implies an alteration in the disposition of the semitones, by increasing or diminishing the number of flats or sharps. It is of two kinds, natural and unnatural. See Chromatic successions, page 21.

1st. Natural modulation, in this work, signifies the going into such keys as are most immediately related to the original key of the piece or movement, *viz.*, the keys of the dominant, the subdominant, the relative, and its dominant and subdominant keys.

Thus, for example, the keys into which a natural modulation may be made, from the major key of C, are G major, the dominant; F major, the subdominant; A minor, the relative minor; E minor, its dominant; and D minor, its subdominant.

And thus from A minor, the natural modulations are into E minor, the dominant; D minor, the subdominant; C major, the relative major; G major, its dominant; and F major, its subdominant. In other words, the keys thus intimately related, have only one flat or sharp, more or less, than the original key. And these keys are also represented by the chords Do,

Fa, and Sol, of the original and relative keys, being those which may be used together in the same diatonic scale. Thus in the diatonic scale of naturals, the chords which may be used without changing the scale, answer to the names of the keys into which a natural modulation may be made: *viz.*, C major, G major, F major, A minor, E minor, and D minor.

2nd. Unnatural modulation, in this work, signifies modulation into any keys not intimately connected (as above) with the original key: or, in other words, into such keys as have more than one flat or sharp, more or less, than the original key, and which cannot be represented by the triads of Do, Fa, and Sol, of the major and relative minor keys.

Thus, for example, a modulation from C major, into the keys of C minor, G minor, F minor, A major, E major, D major, B minor, B flat major, &c., is, in this work, called unnatural. So also, from A minor into A major, E major, D major, C minor, G minor, F minor, &c.

Chromatic modulation, whether natural or unnatural, may be effected in two different ways—by gradual and by sudden modulation.

1st. Gradual modulation signifies such as is effected by doubtful chords, or chords common both to the original key and to that into which the modulation is made.

Major triads are doubtful chords, as in Example 362, where the third and fourth chords may be either Sol, Do, in the key of C major, or Do, Fa, in G major. See also Examples 363, 364, 365, and 366.

The triad of *Fa*, in the minor key, may be converted into Fa with a sixth and third in the major key. See pages 29 and 41; and Examples 367 and 368.

Fa in the minor key, with a sixth and third (the fifth being understood), may be converted into Re with a sixth and third in the major key (the fourth being understood), as in Examples 369 and 370.

F

The leading seventh in the major key, is convertible into the added sixth in the minor key inverted, as a seventh fifth and third.   Example 371.

The Neapolitan sixth is also a doubtful chord.

All doubtful chords are determined, in this work, by the succeeding chords which are not doubtful; especially in music composed in time, when the change of key is supposed to take place as soon as possible after the preceding cadence.   See Example 372, where the chords which are doubtful are noticed; also in Examples 373 and 374.

2nd.   Sudden modulation means such as passes from one key to another by chords which are not doubtful, but decidedly in another key, as in Example 375.

In modulation it will be advisable for the composer to be guided in his choice of the first chord of the new key by the rules of the diatonic succession.   Thus, after a close in the major key of c, if the composer wishes to go into E minor, he should consider whether *Do*, *Fa*, or *Sol*, of E minor would be the best chord to begin with, *viz.*, whether it would be better to go

> From the triad of c to that of E, *Do*, rising a 3rd.
> From   ..   c   ..   A, *Fa*, falling a 3rd.
> Or from   ..   c   ..   B, *Sol*, falling a 2nd.

Example 376; and he would prefer *Fa*, falling a third, from the rules given, page 20.

Order and Duration of Modulation.

The order of modulation from a major key is usually,
> 1st, Into the dominant;
> 2ndly, Into the subdominant;

3rdly, Into the relative;

4thly, Into the subdominant of the relative;

5thly, Into the dominant of the relative.

After any or all of these, a return may be made to the original key, at the option of the composer.

From a minor key the modulations, in ancient music, were the same as from a major key. But in modern music the order is sometimes as follows:

1st, Into the relative major key;

2ndly, Into the subdominant of the original key;

3rdly, Into the dominant;

4thly, Into the subdominant of the relative;

5thly, Into the dominant of the relative.

But the modulation of modern music is scarcely subject to any rule.

The duration of each key, in general, corresponds, in some measure, with the order of modulation. A piece of music remains some considerable time in the original key at its commencement and conclusion; and, as a return to it may be made after each or any of the modulations, it, of course, occupies more of the composition than any of the other keys. The key into which the first modulation is made, is generally next in duration, and the other keys take up a comparatively short portion of the composition.

Transient modulation is such, whether diatonic or chromatic, as is of very short duration. See Examples 377 and 378.

The keys of which the various movements of an Oratorio, Opera, Sonata, Concerto, or other long composition consist, should, in general, be related to each other; or, in other words, the change of key from one movement to another should be natural, excepting where an effect is to be produced, corresponding with the change of scene, or for the sake of contrast. In modern music, however, this connexion is frequently disregarded.

F 2

Modulation by discords of Syncopation.

In discords of Syncopation (Example 308), after the discord of Fa, inverted as a seventh fifth and third on Re, the bass may fall a fifth to Re, in the key of the subdominant, with a seventh fifth and third (Example 379), and this may again fall a fifth, &c., as often as the composer pleases. Examples 380 and 381.

Modulation by a succession of Dominant Sevenths.

The Dominant seventh may be resolved by the bass note Sol falling a perfect fifth to another dominant seventh, and so on as long as the composer pleases. Example 382.

In accompanying this, the leading note (instead of rising) must fall one semitone to the next discordant note.

Modulation by a succession of Diminished Sevenths.

The leading note, when accompanied by a diminished seventh, may (instead of rising) fall a semitone, and be accompanied with a sixth, sharp fourth, and flat third (*viz.*, an inversion of a leading seventh), and so on alternately, as in Example 383.

The diminished seventh may be either on the leading note, or on Fa sharp. See Chromatic Discords.

This passage sometimes rises instead of falling a semitone.

III. Enharmonic Modulation signifies either, 1st, the passing from one discord to another of the same sound, on a keyed instrument, but expressed by different notes in writing.   Example 384.

Or rather, 2ndly, The resolution of a discord as if it consisted of other notes, which produce the same sound on keyed instruments.

Thus the diminished seventh in the key of c $\begin{smallmatrix} A\flat \\ F \\ D \\ B \end{smallmatrix}$ may be resolved as if it

consisted of $\begin{smallmatrix} G\sharp \\ F \\ D \\ B \end{smallmatrix}$ or $\begin{smallmatrix} A\flat \\ F \\ D \\ c\flat \end{smallmatrix}$ Example 385.

Thus the Dominant seventh may be resolved as if it were the German sixth.   Example 386.

The seventh and third on Sol as if it were the Italian sixth.   Example 387.

And the diminished seventh on Fa$\sharp$, as if it were an inversion of the diminished seventh on _Re_.   Example 388 *.

The student is particularly recommended, before he proceeds further, to make himself well acquainted with all the preceding part of this work ; examining for himself the works of good composers ; and adopting whatever he admires in their method of treating discords and modulation.

---

* For-Examples of Enharmonic Modulation, see the Recitatives, ' Thy Rebuke,' in the Messiah; ' My genial spirits droop,' Samson ; the second part of the air, ' Return, O God of Hosts,' Samson ; and the conclusion of the chorus, ' The Heavens are telling,' in Haydn's Creation : the derivation of which will be seen, Examples 389, 390, 391, and 392.

CHAPTER VII.

OF CANON, FUGUE, AND IMITATION.

A CANON is a melody performed by two or more parts of a score at the same time *, subject to all the foregoing rules of harmony and music in real parts.

Canons are either 2 in 1, *viz.*, two parts performing the same melody †.

Or, 3 parts in 1 melody.

4, 5, 6, or any number

in 1 . . . .

4 in 2 melodies.

5 in 2, *viz.*, 3 in 1 and 2 in the other.

6 in 2 melodies.

7 in 2, *viz.*, 4 in 1 and 3 in the other.

8 in 2 . . . .

6 in 3 . . . .

8 in 4 . . . .   &c. &c.

The principal melody (or that which begins) is called the subject ; the

---

* *Viz.*, one part must begin before the other has concluded.

† A canon originally signified a kind of musical puzzle, or enigma. In a canon of two in one, or more in one, only one line was written, and the student, by way of musical exercise, was to discover the method of performing, or, as it is called, of solving, the canon. In a canon of four in two, six in two, or eight in two, only two lines were written, &c. Example 411.

[120]

Ex: **404.** Canon 6 in 3 8ᵛᵉ below

Ex: 405. Canon 6 in 2 8ve and 15th below

Coda

Ex: 414.

Ex: 415.

Ex: 416.

Ex: 417.

subject or answer.

answer or subject.

Ex: 418.

Ex: 419.

answer or subject

subject or answer

Ex: 420.

Ex: 421.

Ex: 422.

Ex: 423.

Ex: 424.

Ex: 425.

Ex: 426.

Ex: 427.

The second Strain is the same melody performed backwards.

Solution, or the 2.^d Strain, obtained by performing the above melody backwards.

Ex: 428.

Ex: 429. Solution of the foregoing melody.

Ex: 430.

Ex: 431.

Solution of the foregoing melody.

Ex: 432.

D.C.

D.C.

Ex: 433.

Ex: 438.

Handel

others are called the answers : these may begin on the unison (*viz.*, on the same note with which the subject begun), on the octave or fifteenth above or below the note with which the subject begun ; on the fourth or eleventh, above or below ; on the fifth or twelfth, above or below ; or on any other note which the composer may choose : but the above-mentioned canons are recommended as most easy of construction. These particulars are generally specified at the beginning of the canon. Thus a canon, two in one, on the unison, signifies that two parts perform the same melody, both beginning on the same note ; three in one on the fifth and eighth above, means that three parts perform one melody, the answers beginning respectively a fifth, and an octave, above the first note of the subject.

For a Canon, two in one on the unison, see Example 393 *.

In making this, and all other canons, the composer, after writing as much of the subject as exists before the answer begins, suppose one bar, marked (1), is to transcribe it, before he goes any further, into the answer marked (2) ; then he may compose a similar portion, as the bar marked (3), making it a good accompaniment to bar (2) ; then transcribe it to bar (4) ; then add (5), (6), (7), &c. &c. The length of this portion, or distance, at which the answer is made, is at the option of the composer. If very distant, the canon is so extremely easy of construction as to possess little merit ; and if too near, the subject will not be distinguished by the ear, before its answer commences. See Examples 394 and 395.

Example 396 is a canon 2 in 1 on the 8ve below.

	397		2 in 1	..	8ve above.
..	398	..	3 in 1	..	unison.
..	399	..	3 in 1	..	8ve and 15th below.

* This and many other canons marked, &c., at the end, are purposely left unfinished, that the student may complete them.

Example 400 is a canon 3 in 1 on the 8ve and 15th above.

..   401   ..   3 in 1   ..   8ve below and 8ve above.

..   402   ..   4 in 1   ..   unison.

..   403   ..   4 in 2   ..   8ve below; here are 2 subjects and 2 answers.

..   404   ..   6 in 3   ..   8ve below, *viz.*, 3 subjects and 3 answers.

..   405   ..   6 in 2   ..   8ve and 15th below, *viz.*, 2 subjects and 4 answers.

..   406   ..   2 in 1   ..   12th above.

Previously to the composition of a canon, in which the answer is to be on the fifth, twelfth, fourth, or eleventh, above or below, in which there is to be no modulation, the student is recommended to write the scales of each part, one over the other, the intervals being exactly the same in each, as in Example 407 ; and observe which note of the subject will cause an alteration of flats and sharps in the answer, in order that it may be avoided. Thus, if the canon is to be on the fifth or twelfth above, or the fourth or eleventh below, the seventh note of the key should be avoided in the subject, because it produces an accidental sharp in the answer : and if the canon be in the fifth, or twelfth below, or the fourth or eleventh above, the fourth note of the subject is to be avoided, because it will produce an accidental flat in the answer. But if the composer wishes to modulate, he may use these or any other notes. See Example 408, which is a canon two in one, on the fifth above, with modulation.

Example 409, is a canon two in one, on the fifth below, without any modulation.

Example 410, is a canon two in one on the twelfth below, with modulation.

[144]

A perpetual canon is one in which a certain number of bars are marked to be repeated as often as the performers choose, (which is usually three times,) and then the canon is concluded, either by a pause over one of the notes, as in Example 411; by a double bar, as in Example 412; or by a coda, as in Example 413, *viz.*, a few bars, either in canon or not, as the composer pleases.

A canon which is not perpetual usually terminates with a few bars or notes not in canon, as Example 414.

Example 415 is a canon three in one on the fourth and eighth below; and Example 416 is a canon three in one, on the fifth and fifteenth below.

A canon by inversion * is one in which the answer consists of the same melody as the subject, but all the motion inverted. Where the subject ascends the answer is to descend, and *vice versâ,* the intervals remaining strict : *viz.*, if the subject ascends a major third, the answer must descend a major third ; if the subject descends an imperfect fifth, the answer must ascend a similar interval, &c. Previous to the composition of this sort of canon the student should make a scale, as before, of the subject and answer, the one ascending, the other descending by similar intervals, as in Example 417, where it will be found that when the subject begins on the key note of the major key, an answer on the third or tenth above, or on the sixth or thirteenth below, will be the most easy to construct. Example 418 is a canon two in one by inversion on the sixth below. Example 419 is another preparatory arrangement of scales, in which the subject may begin on the key note of the minor key, and the answer on the seventh or four-

---

* This sort of canon has also been called *per arsin et thesin ;* and, by the Italians, *moto contrario.* Inversion here relates to the motion of the notes, not to the position of the parts —as in an interval inverted, or a counterpoint inverted, where the bass becomes the treble, and the reverse.

[145]

teenth above; or it might be on the second or ninth below. Example 420 is a canon two in one, by inversion on the fourteenth above.

A canon by augmentation is one in which the notes of the answer are double the length of those in the subject. The answer may begin either with or after the subject. Example 421 is a canon, two in one, by augmentation, on the fifteenth below.

Double augmentation signifies that the notes of the second answer are twice the length of those of the first answer, and four times the length of those of the subject.

Example 422 is a canon, three in one, by augmentation and double augmentation, on the unison and fifteenth below.

A canon by diminution signifies one in which the notes of the answer are half the length of those in the subject, as in Example 423, which is a canon two in one, by diminution, on the octave above.

Double diminution signifies that the notes of the second answer are one quarter of the length of those in the subject. Example 424 is a canon three in one, by diminution, and double diminution, on the octave above.

A canon in which the intervals are not exactly preserved in the answers, is not, in this work at least, considered as strict. In some pieces called canons, however, it has been thought sufficient that the answer should be in the same key.

Example 425 is a canon three in one, on the ninth and tenth above, the intervals not being regarded.

A canon may have one or more parts of free accompaniment, *viz.*, not in canon.

Example 426 is a canon two in one, on the fifth above, with a free bass.

Passages in strict canon are frequently introduced in fugues, choruses, symphonies, quartetts, and all kinds of music.

[146]

Other pieces of music, besides those of the foregoing description, have obtained the name of canons; but they do not answer the definition adopted in this work, *viz.*, that a canon is ' a melody performed by two or ' more parts of a score at the same time.'

Such are melodies that are first played forward and afterwards backward. The melody in two parts, Example 427, is to be first performed in the usual manner from left to right, and then from right to left, or *per recte et retro.*

It is evident that this is not the same melody performed by two or more parts of a score at the same time; and, therefore, if written in such a manner as to appear like a canon, it will not, nevertheless, be deserving of the name: yet this sort of composition has been so written, by transferring the under part of the solution to the same line with the upper melody, as in Example 428; and it has then been called a canon two in one, *per recte et retro, viz.,* two parts in one line; the one reading from left to right, and the other, *at the same time,* from right to left.

A melody *alla rovescio* is one which is first performed in the usual way, and then with the paper inverted, as in Example 429. This evidently is not the same melody, performed by two or more parts of a score at the same time; yet this kind of composition also has been written in the form of a canon, as in Example 430, and been called canon two in one, *alla rovescio.*

The name of canon has also been bestowed on such a melody as Example 431, which is first to be performed in the usual way, from left to right, and then from right to left; then the paper is inverted, and the melody performed from left to right, and from right to left: this, however, not producing a full close, the paper must be returned to its former position, and the melody again performed from left to right, and from right to left; and this has been called a canon three in one, *per recte et retro*, and *alla rovescio*.

Rounds, also, or catches, have been written in the form of canons, and called such, particularly by the modern Italians.

A Round is a vocal composition in three or more parts, all written in the same clef, the performers of which are to sing each part in succession, as is indicated by the figures at the beginning and end of each line, *viz.*, the first voice is to sing the first, second, and third parts in succession, and then the first again, &c. The second voice is to begin the first line when the first voice begins the second; and when the first voice begins the third line, the third voice is to begin the first line, and the second voice the second line. See Example 432

That this does not answer the definition of a canon is obvious; yet it is frequently made to resemble a canon in unison, by writing it at length, as in Example 433.

Rounds are also written in the form of canons, the voices answering in octaves instead of unisons. Still these are only rounds in disguise.

Of Fugue.

A strict Fugue is a composition in which a subject, given out by one of the parts in the authentic mode, is answered in the plagal, and *vice versâ*. All fugues, in which this rule is not observed, will, in this work, be considered as free, *viz.*, not strict fugues.

The authentic Mode is that part of the key contained between the key note, Do, and its fifth above, Sol; and the plagal mode is the remaining part, contained between Sol and the key note, Do, above Sol. Thus the authentic mode consists of five notes, and the plagal of four.

The above is said to have originated in the Chants of the old Christian church.

In the commencement of a strict fugue, the extreme notes Do and Sol of the authentic mode are to be respectively answered by the extreme notes Sol and Do of the plagal, and *vice versâ*, the intermediate notes not being liable to any rule.

> Thus Do is answered by Sol,
> Re . . . . by La,
> Mi . . . . by Si,
> Fa and Sol . . by Do. Ex. 434.
> Or, Do and Re . . by Sol,
> Mi . . . . by La,
> Fa . . . . by Si,
> And Sol . . . . by Do. Ex. 435.

In the minor key, *La* and *Si* in the plagal modes may occasionally be raised a semitone. Example 436.

In a strict fugue every subject begins either with Do or Sol.

Example 437 contains a variety of subjects with their answers. In general, however, it is sufficient that the above rules be attended to in the two first notes of the subject, and the rest of the answer may be considered as in the dominant key, like the answer of a canon on the fifth above, or fourth below.

In a strict fugue the subject is given out by one of the parts, then the answer is made by another; and afterwards the subject is repeated by a third part; and if the fugue consists of four parts, the answer is again made by the fourth part; after which, the composer may use either the subject or the answer, or small portions of them, in any key he pleases, or even on different notes of the key.

In Example 438 the empty bars marked thus (&c.), contain any free accompaniment the composer pleases ; but, of course, the more it resembles the style of the subject the better, unless intended for contrast. See also Examples 439 and 440, where this sort of accompaniment is inserted in little notes. Between the subjects, or between the subjects and the answers, and *vice versâ*, some passage, perhaps not necessarily resembling the subject, may be used to assist the modulation and introduce a return of the subject, as Example 441.

The answers and subjects of a fugue should become more close and frequent (*piu stretto*) towards its conclusion.

A subject which can only be performed by one part at a time is unfit for a fugue, rendering it tedious and uninteresting.

Example 442 is a subject with its answers and repetitions, at various distances of time, and on various notes of the key.

The first note of the subject or answer is frequently shortened or lengthened in the course of the fugue, as in Examples 443 and 444.

A double Fugue is one in which there are two or more subjects, some two of which, at least, are used together in the course of the fugue.

The subjects may either begin nearly together, at the beginning of the fugue, as in examples 445, 446, and 447 ; (where they are distinguished by the figures 1st and 2nd;) or the second subject may be introduced in the middle, or towards the latter end of the fugue ; either by itself, as in Example 448, or together with the first subject, as in Example 449.

Example 450 exhibits the four subjects of the chorus ' Let old Timotheus yield the prize,' in Handel's Alexander's Feast.

The subject of a fugue is sometimes answered in inversion, reversion, diminution, and augmentation, as in canons.

The subject is answered in inversion in the fugue of Handel's Overture to Esther. Example 451.

In the last movement of Handel's Oratorio of the Messiah the subject is answered by reversion, which is very uncommon in fugues. See Example 452, where the bars are omitted purposely, for the sake of avoiding a dissimilitude in the notation, which would render the contrivance less apparent.

Example 453 is an answer by diminution from the chorus 'Let all the Angels of God,' from the Oratorio of the Messiah. See note on Counterpoint, page 56.

Example 454 is an answer by augmentation.

A holding note, or pedale, may be used either on Sol or Do in the bass, and sometimes first on one and then on the other, for several bars immediately previous to the conclusion of a fugue. See Example 455 from the last movement in the Oratorio of the Messiah. This passage has also been called a *point d'orgue*, as well as *pedale*, having originated in the use of the pedals attached to the lower notes of many church organs, particularly on the continent.

Of Imitation.

By Imitation, in this place *, is meant the resemblance between the melodies of the several parts of a score, in a less strict way than that of a canon or fugue ; and which exists, more or less, in the scientific music of every age ;

---

* Imitation also signifies the endeavour of conveying an idea of storms, battles, waves, the singing of birds, ringing or tolling of bells, &c., by musical notes. This has often been absurdly extended to such objects in nature as have no sound, as the rising sun, lightning, snow, &c. See the Author's *Lectures on Music.*

[151]

excepting when the whole attention is intended to be directed to the principal melody, in which case alone such a bass and accompaniments as would suit one piece of music as well as another are admissible.

Under this head may be arranged all canons and fugues which are not strict throughout.

Chapter VIII.

OF VOCAL AND INSTRUMENTAL MUSIC.

THE specimens hitherto adduced, and the compositions which the student has attempted (excepting rounds), may be considered as equally fit for either vocal or instrumental music, and a great deal of the best productions of all ages is thus doubtful in its character. Instrumental music is sometimes so smooth and vocal, that words might easily be adapted to it; and vocal music is frequently so decidedly expressive, that when sung to an unknown language, or performed on instruments, no aid of words seems requisite.

The expression of words is a subject which, perhaps, need not engross the first thoughts of the young composer, and which the author of the present treatise intends to consider, together with other subjects equally connected with taste, in another work *. But it is conceived that a list of voices and instruments, with their compasses and cliffs, will be found useful to the student in the present state of his progress.

The student should be particularly careful in the manner of accenting his words in vocal music; and, for this purpose, he should mark them with long and short accents, observing that the most strongly accented syllables should fall on the beginning of the bar.

Voices are of four kinds,—treble, alto, tenor, and bass. Treble voices are of two kinds: the treble clef will show the scale of the high treble voice, and the tenor clef on the first line that of the low treble or mezzo

* Lectures on Music, since published.

G

soprano, according to the following rule, which will apply for general purposes to all clefs, but which is not applicable to songs, for which, indeed, no certain rule can be given.

General rule.   The scale of a voice written in its own peculiar clef may extend from the first line of the stave to the first ledger line above.

See Example 456 for the treble, canto, or soprano voice ; Example 457 for the low treble, canto secondo, or mezzo soprano. See Example 458 for the alto, contralto, or counter tenor. See Example 459 for the tenore, or tenor ; and Example 460 for the basso, or bass.

Instruments may be divided into :—

    1st. Keyed instruments.

    2nd. Stringed instruments.

    3rd. Wind instruments.

    4th. Instruments of percussion.

1st. Of keyed instruments there have been many kinds, as organs, clavichords, virginals, spinets, harpsichords, and piano-fortes ; of these only the organ and piano-forte are at present generally used.

All organs contain, at least, four octaves, (*viz.*, five notes called c, as in Example 461,) including semitones, though the number of notes below or above the lowest and highest c is uncertain.   The lowest c♯ is made A on organs which have short octaves, and then the note B, below it, is made G, and the scale commences as in Example 462.

The most suitable passages for the organ are those which consist of slow and holding notes ; distinct or quick passages should only be used for the sake of contrast, and passages of execution should be almost entirely excluded *.

  * In composing for keyed instruments, the number of notes which the hand can grasp should be considered.

[154]

As organs are at present tuned, (with unequal temperament,) keys which have many flats or sharps will not have a good effect, especially if the time be slow.   Harpsichords in general, and piano-fortes as they were originally made, without additional keys, contain six notes called F, or five octaves, as in Example 463.   Piano-fortes with additional keys above, ascend to C; and those with additional keys below begin from C, and contain six octaves. Examples 464 and 465 *.

The peculiar characteristic of the harpsichord was clearness, or precision. That of the piano-forte, (as its name implies,) is its power of varying the degrees of loudness and softness, either suddenly or by the crescendo, diminuendo, rinforzando, &c.

2nd.   Stringed instruments played with the bow consist at present of violins, tenors, violoncellos, and double basses.

For the scale and clef of the violin, see Example 466 †.

In solos and solo concertos the violin scale may extend an octave higher, but this is a species of music which no young composer should attempt, unless he is himself a performer on the instrument for which he writes.

In scores there are generally two violin parts.

Stringed instruments, played with the bow, are superior in point of expression to keyed instruments, as they combine the sostenuto of the organ, the precision of the harpsichord, and the variety of power of the piano-forte; and are also capable of producing the smallest intervals.

The tenor, or *alto viola,* is a larger kind of violin; or, to speak more cor-

---

* Since the first publication of this work the scale of piano-fortes has been extended.

† In composing for stringed instruments, such chords, or double stops, must not be used as cannot be executed. The student may acquire his knowledge of these either by consulting a performer, or by avoiding all passages for which he can find no authority in the works of the great masters.

G 2

rectly, the violin is a diminutive viola or viol. Its scale and clef may be seen, Example 467.

For the scale and clef of the violoncello, see Example 468. This scale, in solos, may be extended upwards considerably.

The usual compass of the double bass is shown in Example 469, but it is written an octave higher than it is intended to be played. In general, however, a separate part is not composed for the double bass, but the performer looks out of the violoncello book, playing the same notes an octave lower, or omitting such notes as he thinks proper. The words *solo violoncello* and *tutti bassi* are used to show when these instruments are to play separately, and when together; but separate lines, and an occasional difference in the passages, are rather recommended *.

3rd. The principal wind instruments now in use are flutes, oboes, clarionets, bassoons, horns, trumpets, and trombones.

For the scale of the German flute, see Example 470. Its principal key is D major with two sharps, and other keys are proportionably unfit for the instrument as they are further removed from this key. The most proper passages for the flute are sweet and soft melodies. In full parts high and lengthened notes are given it in modern music; and, indeed, the general use of wind instruments in the full parts of modern music, is to sustain the principal or essential notes of the harmony, and to supply the want of voices or of the organ †.

---

* The harp is a stringed instrument seldom used in concerts, excepting in solo concertos. Its compass very much resembles that of the piano-forte.

† The flauto piccolo is a shrill flute used by Handel to imitate the singing of birds; and by Glück for the howling and whistling of the wind. If written according to the scale of the German flute, it will sound one octave higher.

For the scale of the oboe, see Example 471 ; its principal key is that of C major. Keys which have many flats or sharps should therefore be avoided in solos, but in full music this instrument is used in almost all keys.

For the scale of the clarionet, most frequently used in concerts, called B flat clarionet, see Example 472. Its compass extends lower than is here shown, but that part of its scale is not perfectly in tune. All music for this instrument must be written one note higher than it is intended to be played. Thus the key of B♭ must be written C, &c. Its most agreeable keys are those which have flats. The clarionet is naturally a very powerful instrument, and was originally appropriated to military bands.

Three other kinds of clarionet are used in military bands, besides that above described; one called the C clarionet, a smaller one called the F clarionet, which goes four notes higher, and one in A. In composing for the C and the F clarionets no transposition of notes is required. They are used in military bands. Music for the A clarionet must be written a minor third higher than it is intended to sound. The B flat and A clarionets are the only ones used in concerts, the one for keys which have flats, and the other for keys which have sharps.

For the scale of the bassoon or fagotto, see Example 473. This instrument can play equally well in all the usual keys. It may be used either as a bass to the other wind instruments, or in the tutti parts it may play in unison with the bass stringed instruments.

The horn and trumpet have similar scales. The generator, or key note, is the sound of the whole tube, which, however, is never used, the sounds consisting entirely of the harmonics or notes produced by the aliquot parts of the tube : *viz.*

Do, the octave to the generator, produced by .	$\frac{1}{2}$
Sol, the 12th, or 5th above the last note . . .	$\frac{1}{3}$
Do, the 15th, or 4th above the last note . .	$\frac{1}{4}$
Mi, the 17th, or major third above the last note .	$\frac{1}{5}$
Sol, the 19th, or minor 3rd above the last note .	$\frac{1}{6}$
*Za †, the 21st, or minor 3rd above the last note .	$\frac{1}{7}$
Do, the 22nd, or 2nd above the last note . .	$\frac{1}{8}$
Re, the 23rd, or 2nd above the last note . .	$\frac{1}{9}$
Mi, the 24th, or 2nd above the last note . .	$\frac{1}{10}$
*Fa, the 25th, or minor 2nd above . . .	$\frac{1}{11}$
Sol, the 26th, or major 2nd above . . .	$\frac{1}{12}$
*La, the 27th, or 2nd above	$\frac{1}{13}$

Other notes have been used by respectable composers, but even all the above are not recommended to the young composer, as those marked thus (*) are out of tune on the common horn and trumpet ‡.

For the scale of the horn in the key of c, see Example 474, which is to be written an octave higher than it is intended to be performed.

By the use of crooks the horn is enabled to play also in the keys of G A B♭ D E♭ E and F, see Example 475; yet all the music for the horn is to be written in the key of c, specifying at the beginning of the movement what the key is, as C, D, G, &c.

The horn is capable of such various degrees of piano and forte, that it is used in all kinds of music.

For the scale of the trumpet in the keys of c and D, which are the most

† Za is a name given to this species of flat seventh by some French writers.

‡ Modern horn players attempt to make these notes in tune by inserting the hand into the bole of the horn; and a sliding mouth-piece has been used, with good effect, to the trumpet for the same purpose.

common keys, and those of B♭, E♭, and F, see Example 476. The trumpet is not so often used in soft as in loud music *.

The trombone, or sackbut, has a sliding mouth-piece, and can express any interval. It is of three kinds, alto, tenor, and bass. These may either be in unison with the alto, tenor, and bass voice parts of a full chorus, or, which is far better, may have separate parts written for them. They are capable of producing very good effects both in loud and soft passages.

4th. Instruments of percussion comprehend cymbals, triangles, carillon, or bells, &c.; but the only instrument of this kind now used in concerts are the kettle drums or double drums, of which a pair may be tuned to the bass notes c and g in the key of c, as in Example 477, or to d and a, in the key of d; B♭ and F, in the key of B♭; and E♭ and B♭, in the key of E♭; but the latter two are peculiar to modern music. The same notes are used for double as for kettle drums.

The drum sometimes may be used to mark, by a single note, the commencement of a bar, or to give force to a loud passage, by a continued beating; but the finest effect produced by it is a roll during a pedale note in the bass, or a crescendo.

Music may also be divided into that for the church, oratorio, opera, concert, and chamber.

Church music consists of psalm tunes, chants, services, anthems, and voluntaries.

* The scale of the bugle horn, and indeed of all simple tubes, is similar to that of the horn and trumpet; its generator is usually an octave higher than that of the trumpet, and it can seldom produce more than the five first harmonics. It is not used in concerts.

Since writing this, the bugle has been rendered a perfect instrument by the addition of keys somewhat similar to those of the oboe and clarionet. The corno Inglese and corno di basetto among wind instruments, and the side drum, Prussian drum, and Indian gong, among those of percussion, are very seldom used.

Psalm tunes ought to consist chiefly of semibreves and minims, with very few crotchets or other short notes. The harmony should be very simple, consisting chiefly of concords, with a few of the most simple discords as a fifth and fourth, seventh and third, dominant seventh, added sixth, and such of the simple diatonic successions as the student has been cautioned to avoid in modern music.

The best models for psalms are the oldest, *viz.*, those of the reformers and old English organists *.

Chants are sung in cathedrals to the psalms of the day, and are of two kinds, single and double. Single chants consist of two parts, the first of three and the second of four bars, the whole lasting one verse. The double chant consists of four parts, the first and third of three bars, the second and fourth of four, and the whole lasting two verses. The first and last bars of each part of a chant must consist of semibreves, and the intermediate bars of minims. For an example of a single chant see Example 478, and for a double chant, 479 ; also Specimens, vol. ii. pp. 11 and 44.

Though the number of bars and notes in a chant is so limited, yet great variety may be effected by the aid of canon, fugue, or imitation.

Services consist of the Te Deum and Jubilate, or the Benedicite and Benedictus, Sanctus, Responses, Nicene Creed, Magnificat and Nunc Dimittis, or Cantate Domino, and Deus Misereatur; Burial Service, &c. Boyce's Cathedral Music, especially the first volume, contains the finest specimens of this kind of music.

Services may be either full or interspersed with verses, but the former are recommended as being most decided in style ; verse services very much resembling anthems.

* Examples **372, 373, 375** ; also see *Specimens*, vol. ii , pp. **2** and **3**, and a *Collection of Psalms* edited by the author of this work.

Anthems are either full or verse; the former should be first attempted by the student, as the varieties of the latter are almost endless. Boyce's second volume abounds with fine full anthems, as the third does with verse anthems.

Organ voluntaries should consist of fugues, with introductions for the full organ, upon the model of Sebastian Bach and Handel. Soft movements for the diapason and swell should be slow and sweet, or mournful and pathetic, and may be in the Italian style of the seventeenth century *. English voluntaries for the trumpet, echo, voxhumane, cornet, oboe, and other solo stops, are too often vulgar, trifling, and ridiculous; being equally void of science, taste, and that decorous gravity of style which should ever characterize church music.

Oratorio music consists of an overture with occasional instrumental symphonies, marches, minuets, dances, &c., the vocal part consisting of recitatives, and accompanied recitatives, airs or songs, duets, trios, quartetts, quintetts, semichoruses, choruses, double choruses, &c.

Under the head of oratorios may be comprehended not only sacred dramas, but anthems, services, masses, and all church compositions for a full orchestra, and even secular dramas, not acted, as masques, serenatas, odes, &c.

The opera is a secular drama set to music entirely, and acted. It consists of the same kind of movements as the oratorio, excepting the double chorus. Indeed, the manner in which all choruses are necessarily performed on the stage, precludes the possibility of having science and ingenuity in their contexture.

The music of dances and ballets is capable of being made the most ingenious and playful of the instrumental kind.

* See *Specimens*, vol. ii.; also *Lectures on Music*.

[161]

Concerts consist, generally, of selections from church, oratorio, opera, and chamber music. The only pieces expressly composed for a concert being concertos, solo concertos, symphonies, and occasionally overtures and songs.

A concerto is an instrumental full piece, with occasional solos for particular instruments. Solo concertos (sometimes called violin concertos, organ concertos, &c.) are intended to display the powers of particular single instruments, with accompaniments for a full band.

The overtures of Bach, Abel, Van Maldere, &c., were similar to the opera overtures of the same period, consisting, generally, of three movements; but the modern concert symphony consists, generally, of four or five movements.

Concert songs differ in no respect from oratorio or opera songs.

Chamber music may be divided into vocal and instrumental. The former consists of cantatas, canzonets, or other songs, with an accompaniment for the piano-forte, harp, violoncello, or, at most, two or three instruments; also of duets, trios, madrigals *, or glees, rounds, canons, &c. The latter consists of sonatas for the piano-forte, with or without accompaniments; duets, for two performers on the piano-forte; solos, for the violin, violoncello, &c., with an accompaniment for the piano-forte or violoncello; duets for violins, &c., trios, quartetts, quintetts, &c. Of these the young composer is recommended to prefer for his own study, madrigals and quartetts; in writing the former he will make real parts for voices, in the ancient style, and in writing the latter he will make real parts for instruments in the modern style.

---

* A Madrigal is a vocal composition consisting general of more than four parts, the words of which are pastoral. Motetts are set to religious subjects. The modern terms for these are glee, and serious glee.

The student is, lastly, recommended to perform the following tasks :—

1st. To make variations to airs in the manner of different masters, especially in a score of four parts.

2nd. To put different basses to a given treble.

3rd. Different trebles to a given bass.

4th. Different trebles and basses to a given inner part *.

5th. To write accompaniments on a ground bass †.

The student is now left to form his taste by the study of the various styles of music. This is not considered as a proper subject for the present work, which is chiefly intended to enable the student to compose with grammatical correctness ‡.

---

* All these are exemplified in the beautiful air by Haydn, with variations. *Specimens,* vol. iii. p. 143.

† A ground bass is one which consists of a constant repetition throughout a whole movement of the same short subject, with different accompaniments. It has always been recommended as a task for young composers. See *Specimens,* vol. ii., No. 33, p. 24, No. 60, p. 48, No. 100, p. 91.

‡ For further remarks on the various styles of music, see *Lectures on Music* by the author.

CHAPTER IX.

OF THE DERIVATION OF THE SCALE, TUNING, TEMPERAMENT, THE MONOCHORD, &c.

THE derivation of the scale of the major or minor key is a subject upon which many hypotheses have been framed, and which seems likely to continue a matter in dispute. Some authors derive it from that of the harmonics, but the resemblance does not seem sufficiently close to warrant such an hypothesis. See the scales of the horn and trumpet in the preceding chapter.

Tartini, in order to obtain the notes of the major key, takes the three notes Do, Fa, Sol, expressed by the numbers 6, 8, 9, which show the respective proportional number of vibrations of each note, as C, F, and G, in the key of C major; and then adds to each of them the principal or loudest harmonics which they produce, *viz.*, the perfect chord or major third and fifth *. Thus C gives E and G, F gives A and C, and G gives B and D; thus filling up the scale, for which reason a succession of triads falling a fifth has ever been agreeable to the ear, as Sol, Do, Fa; and the numbers 6, 8, 9, and 12 (which express these notes Do, Fa, and Sol, together with the octave to Do,) have ever been famous above all others among the ancients, and

---

* Let any of the lowest notes of a piano-forte, harp, violoncello, or of the diapasons of an organ be struck and continued sounding, an ear accustomed to the experiment will distinctly hear the perfect chord of that note, and probably several of the other less audible harmonics.

[164]

Plate III.

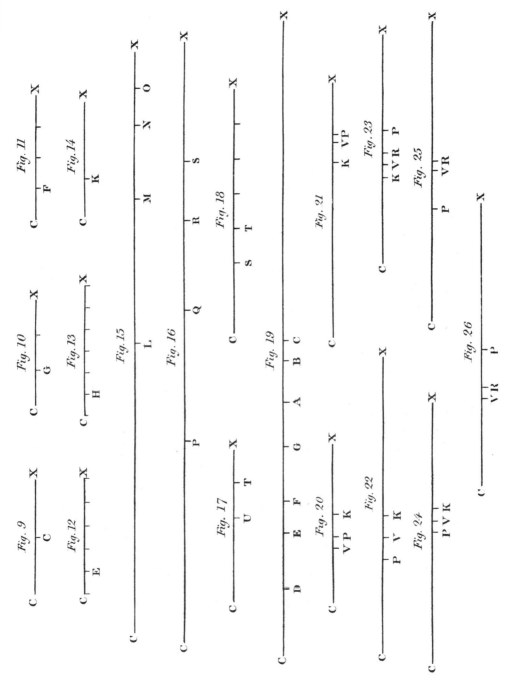

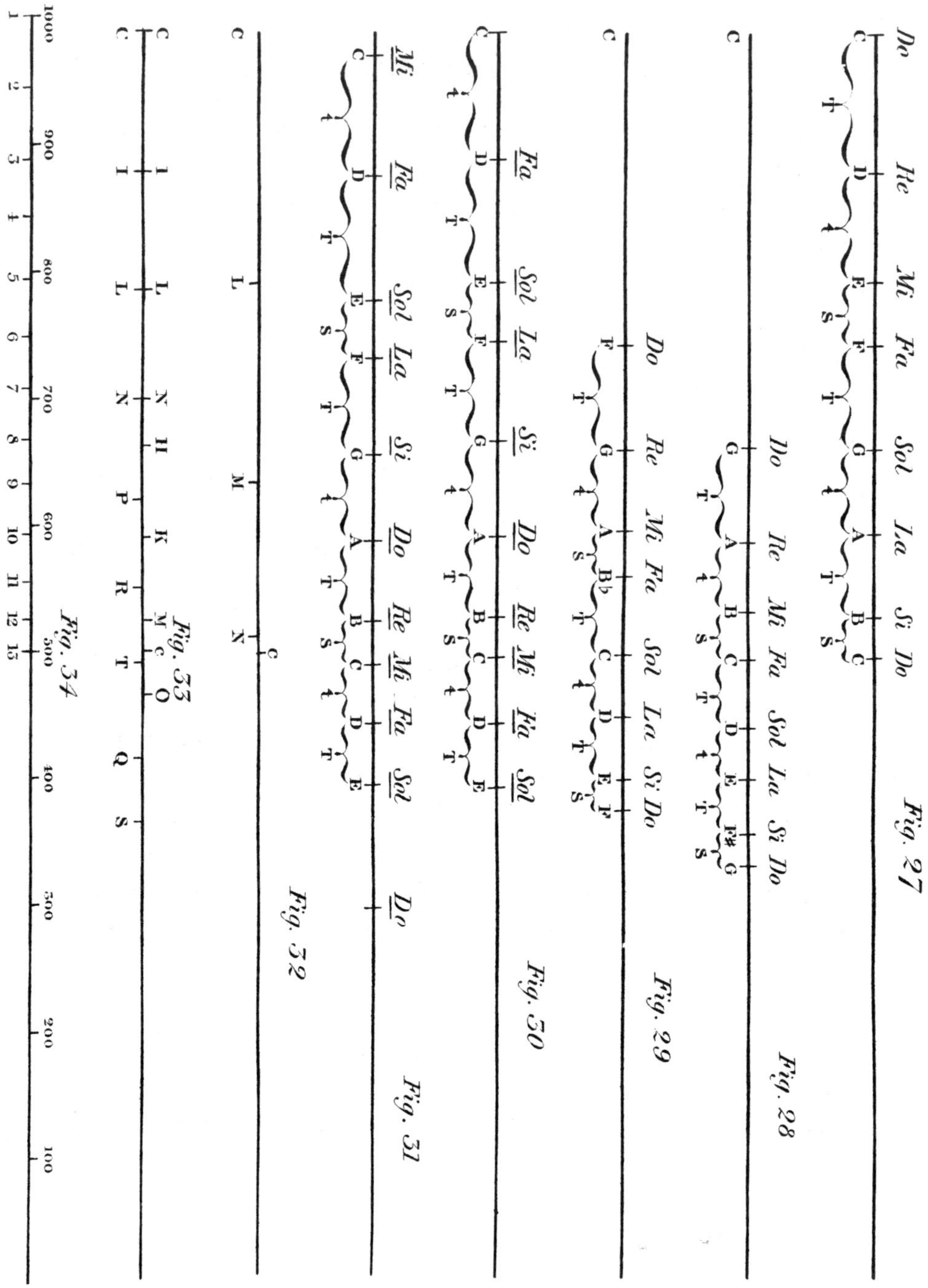

Plate IV

Fig. 27

Do Re Mi Fa Sol La Si Do

Fig. 28

Do Re Mi Fa Sol La Si Do

Fig. 29

Do Re Mi Fa Sol La Si Do

Fig. 30

Fa Sol La Si Do Re Mi Fa Sol

Do

Fig. 31

Mi Fa Sol La Si Do Re Mi Fa Sol

Do

Fig. 32

Fig. 33

Fig. 34

[166]

when tuned by the ear in the following manner, give the major scale as invented by Ptolemy.

Tune the notes G F and E, by the ear, respectively a perfect fifth, perfect fourth, and major third to (*viz*. above) C. Then make A a major third to F, and B a major third to G, and D a perfect fourth below it.

Pythagoras was the inventor of the harmonical canon or monochord, which is merely a string having a board under it of exactly the same length, upon which may be delineated the points at which the string must be stopped to give certain notes. This delineation of ratios renders them capable of being compared, and their respective proportions accurately measured and ascertained.

Figures 6, 7, and 8, plate II, opposite the title, are a section plan and view of a monochord of the most simple construction.

In each of these figures, A B is a board made too thick to warp, having at each end C D, two supports for the string, of which it is required that the internal sides must be perpendicular, and the upper edge not rounded off, that the length of the string and that of the board may exactly correspond; this length is here supposed to be three feet. E is the string which is here supposed to be a steel wire called No. 11. The ends of the wire are attached to a peg at each end, F and G (the latter of which is not visible in figure 8) placed at right angles to the string. Both of these are to be turned in tuning the string, for if only one peg is used the string is apt to stretch more at that end than at the other, and consequently to be inaccurate.

The manner of using the monochord is first to place it on a table, which acts as a sound board to it, augmenting its power. Next tune the string to C, on the second space of the bass clef, by some other instrument, or by a pitch, or tuning fork.   Pinch the string with the finger and thumb * of one hand, taking care not to force the string out of the straight line, and bow on the string with a violin bow in the other.   The student may either mark the board according to his own discoveries of the notes produced by the string, or, which is rather recommended, he may draw lines on the board parallel to the string, and on them mark the places where he is to stop the string in order to produce the notes.

Divide the whole string c x (fig. 9, plate III.) into halves by pinching it at c, the half c x will sound one octave above c x, the whole string.

Divide the whole string c x (fig. 10) into three equal parts, and pinch the string at G, the remaining two thirds G x will give the note G, a fifth to the whole string.

Divide the whole string c x (fig. 11) into four equal parts, and pinch the string at F, the remaining three quarters F x will give the note F, a fourth above the whole string.

Divide the whole string c x (fig. 12) into five equal parts, and pinch the string at E, the remaining four fifths E x will give the note E, a major third to the whole string.

Divide the whole string c x (fig. 13) into six equal parts, and pinch the string at H, the remaining five sixths H x will give the note E♭, a minor third above the whole string.

And in the same way the octave fifth, fourth, major third, and minor third, may be found to any given note on the monochord.

---

* A sliding bridge would doubtless be much more accurate, but also more difficult of performance, and perhaps not necessary for the purposes here required ; namely, of enabling the student to tune, or at least to comprehend the nature of tuning.

Let κ (fig. 14) be the given note; in order to find the octave to κ, consider κ x as a whole string, and divide κ x into two parts, and pinch it so as to take off one of them.

If the fifth to κ is wanted, divide κ x into three parts, taking off one.

If the fourth to κ is wanted, divide κ x into four parts, taking off one.

If the major third is wanted, divide κ x into five parts.

And if the minor third is wanted, divide κ x into six parts.

Thus the octave to c x (fig. 15) is L x, the octave to L is M x, the octave to M is N x, the octave to N is o x, and so on, *ad infinitum*.

In the same way the fifth to c x (fig. 16) is P x, the fifth to P is Q x, the fifth to Q is R x, the fifth to R is s x, &c.

And by reversing the process, the notes below a given note may be found, provided they are not more grave or deep than the generator, or note given by the whole string c x.

To find the octave below a given note T (fig. 17) set off u to the left of T, equal to T x; u x will be the octave below T x.

To find the major third below a given note T (fig. 18) divide T x into four equal parts, and set off T s equal to one of them; s x will be the major third below T x.

In order to tune the major key of c according to the methods of Ptolemy and Tartini, make E a major third to the whole string c x (fig. 19), and G a fifth to it; F a fourth to it, A a major third to F, B a major third to G, D a fourth below G, and c an octave to the whole string.

The point D will be found to be one-ninth of the whole string c x, from c; or rather the note D x is eight-ninths of the whole string c x; and this interval, from c to D, is called a major tone, and it is the difference between a fourth and a fifth; for if a fourth be subtracted from a fifth the remainder will be a major tone.

Thus to find the major tone above any given note v (fig. 20), find к a fifth above v, and р a fourth below к ; р x will be a major tone above v x ; or let v (fig. 21) be the given note, make к a fourth below v, and р a fifth above к ; р x will be a major tone above v x.

But the point е (fig. 19) will not be a ninth part of d x, but a tenth part ; or, in other words, the note е x is not a major tone from d. The interval thus obtained is called a minor tone, and is the difference between a major tone and a major third ; for if a major tone be subtracted from a major third, the remainder will be a minor tone, nine-tenths.

Let it be required to find a minor tone to the given note v (fig. 22), make р a major tone below v, and к a major third to р ; к x will be a minor tone above v x, and will be nine-tenths of v x. Or let v (fig. 23) be the given note, above which it is required to find a minor tone, make р a fourth to v, and к a fifth below р, and, lastly, make r a major third to к, r x will be a minor tone to v x.

If it be required to find the minor tone below a given note v (fig. 24), make к a major tone above it, and р a major third below к ; р x will be a minor tone below v x.

The interval еf (fig. 19) will be found to be one-sixteenth part of the distance е x, *viz.*, f x will be fifteen-sixteenths of е x. The interval is called a major semitone, and is the difference between a major third and a fourth, for if a major third be subtracted from a fourth the remainder will be a major semitone. Thus, let it be required to find the semitone above v (fig. 25), make р a major third below v, and r a fourth above р, r x will be a major semitone higher than v x. Or let v (fig. 26) be the given note, make р a fourth above v, and r a major third below р ; r x will be a semitone higher than v x. If a major semitone is required below a given note, the manner must be reversed. Let r be the given note (fig. 25), make P a fourth below R, and V a major third to P, V X will be a major semitone below R X. Or let R (fig. 26) be the given note, make P a major third to it, and V a fourth below P; V X will be a major semitone below R X *. The interval FG (fig. 19) is a major tone eight-ninths, GA a minor tone nine-tenths, AB a major tone, BC a major semitone. See fig. 27, where the major tones are marked with their usual signature T, the minor tones t, and the major semitones s. It must also be understood,

That a major 3rd is equal to a T and a t as CE

..   minor 3rd   ..   S T   ..   EG

..   perfect 4th   ..   T t s   ..   CF

..   perfect 5th   ..   T T t s   ..   CG

..   major 6th   ..   T T T t s   ..   CA

..   major 7th   ..   T T T t t s   ..   CB

And an 8ve   ..   T T T T t t s s   ..   CC

The minor third DF consisting of t and s, and the fifth DA consisting of T t t s, are therefore not in tune, but are both deficient by a small interval called a comma, which is the difference between a major tone eight-ninths, and a minor tone nine-tenths, and is about as 80 to 81 †.

The note D combined with F or A, however, is not wanted in either of the triads Do, Fa, or Sol of the major key of C, but in the minor key of A the triad of _Fa_ is D F and A : hence a different tuning is required in the

---

* The major or diatonic semitone having been mentioned, it seems necessary to inform the student, that a minor or chromatic semitone (marked s) is the difference between a major semitone and a minor or major tone; as from E♭ to E♮, from c to c♯, from F to F♯, &c. There also several other intervals resulting from the combination of many keys on the same monochord, the knowledge of which is not necessary to the student.

† The ratios of the monochord are generally expressed thus : the major tone $\frac{8}{9}$, minor tone $\frac{9}{10}$, major semitone $\frac{15}{16}$, &c.

H

relative minor key to that just described. But no two major keys at all *related* to each other can exist, on the same keyed instrument, perfectly in tune *. Thus the dominant key of c is g major with one sharp; g will be Do, and a Re, &c., but from Do to Re in a major key ought to be a major tone, see fig. 27; whereas in the major key of c from g to a is a minor tone. Compare figures 27 and 28, the latter of which is the major key of g. And thus in the subdominant of c, f major with one flat, from c to d, *viz.*, from Sol to La should be a minor tone, but in the major key of c, from c to d is a major tone. See fig. 29, and compare it with fig. 27.

The minor key may be tuned likewise in the same way as the major, only making the thirds to *Do*, *Fa*, and *Sol*, minor instead of major. There is some difficulty, however, in choosing the first note *Do* of the principal minor key of a. Some authors make it the same as the note La of the relative major key, *viz.*, a in the key of c, a minor tone above g. In which case all the natural notes excepting d correspond with those of the major key of c. Compare figs. 30 and 27. If the major thirds to *Fa* and *Sol*, f♯ and g♯, be added to this scale, they will be different from those notes in the keys of a major. The author of the present work, therefore, prefers making the key notes of a minor and a major the same; *viz.*, a whole tone from g in the key of c major, see fig. 31, in which case only one natural note of the key of a minor, *viz.*, d, will be the same with those of the major key of c; but the key note, the fifth, and the fourth, will be the same with those of the

---

* In a lecture on this subject, the author of the present work caused the keys of e major with four sharps, and e♭ major with three flats, to be tuned perfectly on the same piano-forte, *viz.*, first the triads of g♯(B) c♯(E) d♯(F♯). And then having two notes, g♯ and d♯ already tuned, which would serve for a♭(E) and e♭(A B), c was added to them, and lastly the triads of g(B♭)(E♭) and d(F)(B♭).

key of A major, three sharps; as also the F♯ and G♯; and also the C♯, which is sometimes used in a close.

Having seen the impossibility of perfection on an instrument which has any limited number of sounds in an octave, the student may next proceed to the study of temperament, *viz.*, of the distribution of the unavoidable imperfection resulting from the limited number of sounds.

On keyed instruments containing only twelve notes in an octave, three major thirds (as CE, EG♯ or A♭, A♭C, or as GB, BD♯ or E♭, E♭G) make an octave; but three major thirds tuned perfectly to each other, as C L M N, fig. 32, fall considerably short of the true octave C. Hence in tuning, one, two, or all of the three major thirds, which constitute every octave, must be tempered too sharp; and the nearer perfection any of them are made, the worse will the others become. N C is the unavoidable imperfection which must be added either to one or more of the thirds, and if equally divided between them will, *upon the whole*, be least offensive to the ear.

Again, twelve fifths, or which is the same thing, six major tones, on a keyed instrument, constitute an octave; but on the monochord it will be found that they exceed it by a small portion, fig. 33, where H I K L M N O P Q R S T represent twelve sounds so obtained, the latter whereof does not coincide with the true octave C: C T is the unavoidable imperfection which must be subtracted from one or more of the twelve fifths which compose an octave. If equally distributed this imperfection will be scarcely perceptible; when the fifths are all equally too flat, the thirds will all become, of their own accord, equally too sharp, and this will render all keys equally imperfect, which is called the equal temperament, and may be obtained on the monochord as follows. Divide the whole string I x into one thousand parts, beginning from right to left, as in fig. 34 :—

[173]

Place the note 2 at 943

.. 　　　　3 .. 890

.. 　　　　4 .. 840

.. 　　　　5 .. 793

.. 　　　　6 .. 749

.. 　　　　7 .. 707

.. 　　　　8 .. 667

.. 　　　　9 .. 629

.. 　　　10 .. 594

.. 　　　11 .. 561

.. 　　　12 .. 529

.. 　　　13 .. 500, the true octave.

Tune any one of the twelve notes of a keyed instrument to the whole string 1—x, then 2—x will give the next note, 3—x the next, &c., to 13—x, which will be an octave to 1—x. If the note 1 x be c, then 2 x will be c♯ or d♭, 3 x will be d, 4 x will be d♯ or e♭, &c. The fifth 8 x will be only one thousandth part of the whole string too flat; but the third 5 x will be seven such parts too sharp.

Unequal temperament is that wherein some of the fifths, and consequently some of the thirds, are made more perfect than on the equal temperament, which necessarily renders others less perfect. Of this there are many systems, which the student is now capable of examining for himself.

He will also find much amusement in studying the various attempts to improve the scale by increasing the number of notes in the octave, such as that of the two additional notes at the Temple organ, of the five additional notes in Mr. Hawke's instruments, and of the twelve additional notes in those by Mr. Löeschman. In all these the bulk, expense, and complication of the instrument are increased in proportion to the number of notes added, and the consequent approach to perfection.

The author, in conclusion, cannot but regret that the preference of English organists for the old method of tuning is (as he is informed) hitherto so strong and determined, as to have resisted and repelled the attempts made to introduce the equal temperament into our Cathedrals and Churches. He has for many years uniformly recommended that this system should have a fair trial, upon the principle that as all tempered fifths and thirds offend the ear, those systems which contain such as are most tempered and most discordant cannot be preferable; especially in an age when the keys which have four sharps and three flats can no longer be excluded from general use. It has at length been fairly tried, and, having carefully examined it, he feels convinced that its practicability and superiority are as unequivocal on the organ as they are allowed to be on the piano-forte, and on all other instruments which contain only twelve different notes in each octave. He continues to press these opinions, not merely because they are his own, but because, in so doing, he is contending for the far higher authority of the judgment and practice of one whom, he trusts, his opponents must venerate and admire,—the greatest of all composers for this sacred instrument—

Sebastian Bach.

LONDON :
Printed by WILLIAM CLOWES,
Duke-street, Lambeth.

[176]

Recently published by Longman, Rees, Orme, Brown, Green, and Longman,
In 8vo., price 7s. 6d. boards,

SUBSTANCE OF SEVERAL COURSES OF LECTURES ON MUSIC,
Read in the University of Oxford, and in the Metropolis.
By W. CROTCH, Mus. Doc., Professor of Music, Oxford, &c.
" We regard this Book as a very pleasant and popular work."—Westminster Review.

LIST OF PUBLICATIONS BY DR. CROTCH,
To be had at the Royal Harmonic Institution, Regent Street.

	£.	s.	d.
Motett, " Methinks I hear," with new instrumental Accompaniments . .	0	4	0
Overture and Finale, La Clemenza di Tito, Mozart, adapted as a Duet for the Piano-forte on a new plan . .	0	3	6
The same, arranged in the usual way .	0	4	0
Sinfonia No. 2, as a Duet, composed by Dr. Crotch . . .	0	7	6
——— No. 7, Salomon's set, Haydn, as a Duet . . .	0	6	0
——— No. 8 . . .	0	6	0
——— No. 10 . . .	0	6	0
Overture, Zauberflöte, Mozart ; Duet	0	3	6
Sinfonia in C (Jupiter), Mozart ; Duet	0	8	0
Nos. 1, 2, 3, 4, 5, constituting the First Act of Don Giovanni, Mozart, for the Piano-forte and Flute, each . .	0	5	0
Ditto, as a Duet, each . .	0	6	0
Preludes for the Piano-forte, and Instructions . . .	0	8	0
Practical Thorough Bass . .	0	12	0
Fugue on a Subject of Three Notes .	0	1	0
Divertimento for the Piano-forte, No. 1	0	2	6
——— No. 2 . . .	0	2	6
——— No. 3			
Anthem, Dr. Greene, " Sing unto the Lord," No. 1 (to be continued) .	0	3	6
Specimens of the various Kinds of Music performed in Dr. Crotch's Lectures, for the Piano-forte, 3 vols., each .	1	5	0
Appendix to ditto, separate .	0	4	0
Palestine, a sacred Oratorio, the words by the late Bishop Heber, the Voice			

	£.	s.	d.
Parts in Score, the Instrumental Parts adapted for the Piano-forte .	2	2	0
The Overture, Choruses, &c., in Palestine, arranged by the Author as Duets for the Piano-forte . .			
Questions in Harmony, with their Answers, for the Examination of Young Pupils . .	0	3	6
Twelve Sinfonias, Haydn ; Piano-forte, with Accompaniments for the Violin and Violoncello, each .	0	5	0
First Concerto, Corelli ; Piano-forte .	0	2	6
" Cruda Sorte," Rossini, as a Duet .	0	3	0
Ditto, single .	0	2	0
Finale to Der Freischutz, Weber .	0	2	6
Finale to the First Act of Il Matrimonio Segreto, Cimarosa, as a Duet .	0	5	0
Coro dello Sbarco, Il Crociato, Meyerbeer ; Duet .	0	3	0
Giovinetto Cavalier, from ditto ; Duet	0	2	0
Sinfonia Kozeluch in F ; Piano-forte, with Accompaniments for the Violin and Violoncello . .	0	5	0
Part of Sinfonia in A, Beethoven ; Duet	0	4	0
Sinfonia Pastorale, Beethoven ; Piano-forte, with Accompaniments for the Violin and Violoncello .	0	10	6
Three Duets, arranged from the Sonatas of Boccherini, as Duets, each .	0	5	0
Airs from Rousseau's Le Devin du Village ; Duet . .	0	4	0
Divertimento, Mozart, from a Quintett in D ; Piano-forte . .	0	3	0
" Cinto di nuovi allori," Rossini ; Duet	0	2	0

OTHER PUBLICATIONS, BY THE SAME AUTHOR.

To be had of Messrs. Lonsdale and Co., Chappell, the Author, &c. &c.

	£.	s.	d.
Three Sonatas	0	7	6
Ten Anthems, in Score	0	10	6
Ode to Fancy, in Score, an Exercise for his Doctor's Degree	1	1	0
Motett, 5 voices, " Methinks I hear "	0	2	6
Glee, 4 voices, " Go, tuneful Bird "	0	1	0
—— 3 voices, " To love thee, O my Emma"	0	1	0
Ode, 5 voices, " Mona on Snowdon calls"	0	2	6
Tallis's Latin Litany and old Psalm Tunes, in Score	0	6	0
No. 1. Original Airs for the Piano-forte, by John and William Crotch	0	2	6
2.	0	2	6
3.	0	2	6
No. 1. Organ Concerto	0	5	0
2. Ditto	0	6	0
3. Ditto	0	7	6
Organ Fugue, on a subject by Muffatt	0	2	0
Glee, 4 Voices, " Nymph, with thee "	0	1	0
Canzonet, " Clear shines the Sky "	0	1	6
Prelude and Air, with Variations; Piano-forte	0	1	6
Glee, 4 voices, " Yield thee to Pleasure"	0	1	6
Sonata, Piano-forte, in E♭	0	4	0
Glee, 5 Voices, " Sweet Sylvan Scenes"	0	1	6
—— 4 Voices, " Hail, all the dear delights"	0	2	0
—— 4 Voices, " Hail, Sympathy "	0	3	0
Air, " Milton Oysters," with Variations; Piano-forte	0	1	6
Fantasia, Piano-forte	0	2	0
No. 1. Concerto, Mozart	0	5	0
2.	0	5	0
3.	0	5	0
Concerto, Dussek (Plough Boy)			
The Overtures, Choruses, Marches, Sinfonias, &c., in Handel's Oratorios, Te Deums, Anthems, Operas, &c.			
No. 1. Esther	0	7	6
2. Deborah	0	7	6
3. Athalia	0	7	6

	£.	s.	d.
No. 4. Acis and Galatea	0	6	0
5. Alexander's Feast	0	7	6
6. Dryden's Ode, " From Harmony"	0	5	0
7. Israel in Egypt	0	10	6
8. L'Allegro ed il Pensieroso	0	5	0
9. Saul	0	10	6
10. Messiah	0	10	6
11. Samson	0	7	6
12. Semele	0	7	6
13. Belshazzar	0	7	6
14. Susanna	0	7	6
15. Six Oboe Concertos	0	10	6
16. Hercules	0	7	6
17. Occasional Oratorio	0	6	0
18. The Choice of Hercules	0	4	0
19. The 12 Grand Concertos, Book I.	0	10	6
20. ——————————— Book II.	0	10	6
21. Joseph	0	7	6
22. Judas Maccabæus	0	10	6
23. Joshua	0	7	6
24. Alexander Balus	0	6	0
25. The 4 Coronation Anthems	0	7	6
26. Solomon	0	10	6
27. Dettingen Te Deum	0	7	6
To be continued.			
Quartett in C, Haydn; Piano-forte	0	3	6
———— in E	0	3	6
Concerto in D, Geminiani; Piano-forte	0	2	0
Sinfonia, by Dr. C. in F, as a Duet, No. 1.	0	8	0
Romberg's Overture in D; Piano-forte	0	2	6
Thirty Rounds for the Piano-forte for learning to play from Score	0	6	0
Duet, The Hope of Israel, 2 Voices	0	2	6
Air, " Twilight," Miss Hammond, with Variations by Dr. C.	0	1	6
" Una bella Serenata," and Finale, Così fan tutte, Mozart, as a Duet on a new plan	0	3	0
" Oh, quanto l'anima," Aria, by Meyer	0	1	6
" Ah, non Sai," Sarti			
" O Lord our Governor," Marcello	0	2	0
Anthem in Score, composed on the Death of the Duke of York	0	10	6